Understanding the
ACT Scientific Reasoning

Understanding the ACT Scientific Reasoning

Jerusha Richardson, B.Sc.

Understanding the ACT Scientific Reasoning

ISBN: 978-1-77136-569-7

Set in 11 point Trebuchet MS by Daria Lacy

Editing by Rosalind Wall

Printed by CreateSpace

I am pleased to hear of any errors, omissions or other feedback on this work. Please contact me at Jerusha@prepACTSAT.com. If you believe I have used your content without authorization, also please contact me.

Dedication

I wrote this book because I know how valuable resources like this are for the many dedicated, hard-working and deserving students out there. Thank you for buying this book; I sincerely hope it helps you.

Acknowledgements

I am very much indebted to Irene Petre, not only for her invaluable feedback on this book, but also for creating a fantastic environment in our tutoring centre, which allowed me to explore and develop the ideas that led to this book.

Likewise, I am grateful to all the students that I've helped with the ACT, both in person and online, because our interactions and your questions led to the creation of this book.

Credit is due to Oliver Alexander, Colleen Reed and Jay Williams for their feedback and advice on this book. I'd like to thank Rosalind Wall, for her copy-editing of this book, and also for her much earlier input into my own reading, writing and reasoning skills. Lastly, I also thank Dave Richardson for always helping me keep things balanced.

One small thing …

Thank you for buying this book. I'm an independent author, so every sale is important to me. If you've enjoyed using this book, please leave me a review on Amazon. You know that everyone who buys on Amazon looks at the reviews, but not many people leave reviews themselves. When you leave a review for my book, it helps other people like you benefit from my advice, and it helps me too! Thanks in advance!

Contents

Introduction

What is the ACT Scientific Reasoning?

The ACT Scientific Reasoning section might be unlike anything you've seen before, but don't be intimidated, even if you haven't done much science in school! It's called scientific reasoning because you have to use your reasoning skills, not your science knowledge!

You have to answer 40 multiple-choice questions, split over six or seven passages. You have 35 minutes for the whole section, which is not a lot of time. Most students can't finish the test in 35 minutes on their first or second try, but by the time they have practiced, they can. Scores on this section tend to be correlated with Reading section scores, as part of the skill tested here is actually reading comprehension. You are not allowed a calculator in the ACT science section.

Each passage has five, six or seven questions, and they fall into three broad categories, which the ACT calls data representation, research summaries and conflicting viewpoints. The conflicting viewpoints passage is very easy to spot: it usually has seven questions and presents the viewpoints of students or scientists who have different ideas about a given topic. There will be one of these in every test. The other five or six passages present data or an experiment that you have to analyze. You might not notice much difference between the data-based passages and the experimental passages – the differences are more subtle. We'll look at the differences later in more detail.

How will this book help me?

In order to succeed at this section, you need three things. I will show you all of these things and help you practice them. You need:

- The right approach – you need to know what to look for in the passage

- The right timing strategies – you need to know when and how to save time

- The right knowledge – basic scientific and mathematical knowledge

First, I'm going to show you the skills that this section is testing. We'll look at why this section even exists in the test and why you need to understand what science is all about. If you understand what the test is asking you to do, it makes the questions much easier!

Once you've worked out how to crack the test, you'll learn how to use your time wisely. I cover all the main timing strategies, the pros and cons of each, and whether you need them or not.

I've given you targeted advice depending on what kind of score improvement you're looking for.

Lastly, there are some chapters that cover the basic knowledge you should have for the test. There are not many questions (1–2 per test) where you need prior knowledge, but knowing the basics can really help you out. Also, there are an increasing number of questions on the Scientific Reasoning section that require you to reason mathematically. I'll tell you how to do that, and explain why you can still get these questions right even if you're not a confident mathematician.

I don't really know anything about the ACT at the moment!

Don't worry! Here's a quick overview. The ACT is a standardized test that is required for admission to most (but not all) universities in the USA. It is designed to test your skills, not your knowledge, in the core areas of English (language use and grammar), mathematics, reading comprehension and scientific reasoning. There is one multiple-choice section for each of those skills. Each one has a different number of questions, but they are all scored on a 1–36 scale. These four scores are then averaged to give you a composite score out of 36. There is also an essay section, which follows the four multiple-choice sections. If you'd like to know more, including the differences between the ACT and SAT, check out the Useful Things appendix, where I discuss this in more detail.

Why did I write this book?

After I'd been tutoring the ACT for a while, I noticed two things. First, I can always finish the scientific reasoning section in about 25 minutes, with fewer than two errors. I'm not superhuman, but I'm obviously better than my students (thankfully!). I am a science graduate, so it makes sense that I'm skilled at this, but once I thought about the reasons why I can do this and my students can't, the idea of this book started to form. Second, I also notice that I can help my students raise their scores quite significantly (often 5+ points) on this section. So how am I helping them? This book aims to give you the advantage of tutoring, without the price tag, and guide you towards the methods of thinking that a trained scientist would use.

I am also a firm believer in giving you the tools you need and letting you decide what works for you. There is no good blanket strategy for any part of the ACT (except really obvious things like: "guess on questions that are taking too long"), so it's important that you get to understand the test and what it's expecting from you so that you can decide which strategies work for you and build your own study plan. Even if you think the ACT is just a meaningless hoop that you have to jump through, the process of diagnosing your weaknesses, constructing a study plan and following through on it is an incredibly valuable skill!

When should I use this book?

This book is designed to introduce you to the Scientific Reasoning section, so use it at the beginning of your prep. Many students do a lot of their prep without really realizing what this section is about, wasting time, sometimes wasting money, and usually increasing frustration. For most students, four months is a good timeframe to prepare for this test, but that does depend on what your score is now, and what you'd like it to be. I talk about coming up with a sensible timeline for your test preparation later in the Useful Things appendix. You probably want to take less than a month to work through everything in this book, and once you've done that, you should spend about three months doing one practice section per week. We'll talk more about this later, but bear in mind that preparing for this test is like learning to ride a bike: it can't be done in a day!

How much do I need to study?

Again, this is something that you'll have a better understanding of once you have worked through this book. The answer is different for everyone – it depends on your score target and how far away that is. You'll have to work this out for yourself, but there is a lot of guidance in this book about how to study and improve your score. However, in my experience, there is a fairly accurate generalization that can be made about someone's progress on the Scientific Reasoning section. Here it is, in graph form (because it's the Scientific Reasoning – what did you expect?!).

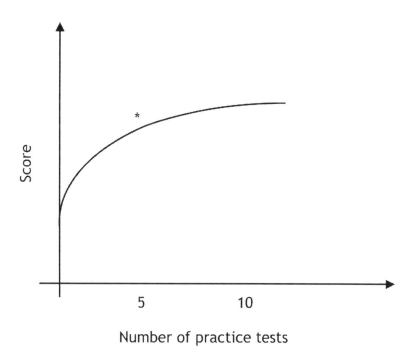

The numbers might differ a little bit from person to person, but what I'm trying to tell you is that there's a very steep initial improvement for your first 3-5 practice tests. After that, it levels off a bit, but you may still continue to improve. Any time after the * is a good time to take the test for real. In other words, you MUST do AT LEAST FIVE practice tests before you write the ACT.

But I don't test well …

I believe that the ACT does what it aims to do reasonably well – it tests your command of written English, mathematics, reading comprehension, scientific reasoning and writing skills. Remember that the test is skill based, not knowledge based. It only reflects one aspect of learning, which is why your GPA and other things are taken into account by universities. There are flaws in any test, and there are some students whose scores don't reflect their aptitude for learning, but generally, the ACT is a reasonable measure of most students' learning skills.

I say this not as a disclaimer, but as advice: if you are not getting the score you think you should be getting after taking several practice tests, consider getting an education professional (such as teacher, counselor or experienced tutor) to work with you and figure out why; many times, a lower score on these tests can help you pinpoint where to improve so that you really are ready for higher education.

I'm not talking about a score that's two or three or even five points lower than you want, but if you're getting a composite 15 when you think you should be getting a 30, you should try to figure out why. If your score on any section is below a 21 and you've done at least three practice tests and gone over your mistakes, it may also be time to get some expert help. You probably need more than a book to guide you, but it's worth putting in the time to improve now. I want to help you prepare for this test, so it's only right that I tell you when you need more tailored advice than a book can give.

For now, thanks for reading this far! Let's get started!

The Approach

What is "scientific reasoning?"

First, what is science? If you asked someone this question, they might say, "Well, science is physics, chemistry and biology," or any number of other scientific fields. But these are only topics that can be understood by scientific methods, they're not science itself!

To understand what's required of you in the ACT Scientific Reasoning section, you should have a good idea of what "scientific reasoning" actually is! Here's a process known as the scientific method.

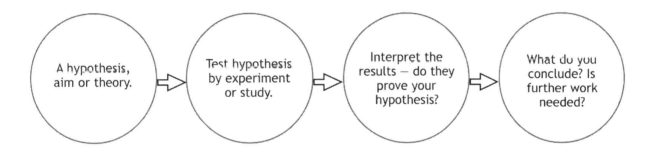

It has developed over many years, and it's based on the idea of falsifiability: that in order to prove something is true, it must be able to be proved false.

For example, the hypothesis: "Usain Bolt is a faster runner than me" is scientific, because it can (and would be!) proven true. We can run a race together, and the winner is the faster one. The hypothesis: "There is a giant octopus-shaped bus somewhere in the universe" is not really scientific, because it can't be proven false – we can't reasonably search the entire universe!

You might be familiar with this process. When you do an experiment you are testing your hypothesis, and interpreting the results (i.e. the second and third stages above). Now, in high school, you are usually given the first two points above, and the result of the experiment is already known. But at some point it wasn't, and so this process has to be followed. This is also roughly the format of a lab report, for the same reasons.

Introducing the HoVerCrafT strategy

So how does this help me understand the ACT Scientific Reasoning?

Those stages of the scientific method above give you key things that you should be able to pick out of each passage. As you read the passage, you should be able to identify:

hypothesis   variables   trends   conclusions

Now, HVCT is not very memorable, so I've called this the HoVerCrafT strategy. I'll keep reminding you of this strategy by using this little picture:

Before you begin each passage, write HoVerCrafT at the top, or draw a little hovercraft if you're feeling creative (but don't waste time). Now, as you read, do the following:

- Make sure you know the hypothesis (underline the sentence that's the closest to a hypothesis). If you can't find a single sentence, just jot down the aim of the experiment. Sometimes it's just a topic, especially on the data representation passages.

- Identify the variables - circle them in passages and graphs. You'll always find the variables on the axes of graphs. Make sure you know which ones the experimenters are controlling (independent variables), and which ones they are measuring (dependent variables). For example, changing temperature to see how it affects density makes T the independent variable and density the dependent variable. Many passages contain more than one experiment, so make sure you identify which variable changes between experiments. If you're still a little confused about variables, I'll go over this again on page 22.

- If there are any tables, see if there is a trend in the numbers (if they are increasing or decreasing). Draw an arrow in the table to represent the direction of the change. This way, you can see very easily if one variable increases while another decreases.

- Find the conclusion. This may be given somewhere in the passage, or you may have to identify it yourself. If you can't identify it quickly, it's OK to skip this one and move to the questions.

These four points are the skills that the passage is trying to test, and they often do it by using a type of experiment or situation you've never seen before, to make it harder. If you've done a practice test already, you've likely figured out that it's quite hard to finish it in 35 minutes. That's because you're being presented with a lot of information, and it's hard to know what's relevant and what's not. Those four points (**hypothesis, variables, trends, conclusions**) are the key information.

When you complete this section, you shouldn't be aiming to read every single word of the whole passage! Instead, use HoVerCrafT to pick out the key points. The conflicting viewpoints section is slightly different, so we'll cover that separately in a few pages. You'll always have H and V. You'll sometimes have T; it depends on how the data is presented to you. You may be able to find C as well. It's ideal if you do, but also may take too much time. Sometimes answering the questions helps you figure out the conclusions, so don't stress on this one.

At this point, you might be thinking: "I've been doing the Scientific Reasoning section already, and I don't do this." In fact, usually about 15 questions per test ask you directly about the **hypothesis, variables, trends or conclusions,** so you have probably been thinking along these lines. Consciously employing this method will help you save time and get a better understanding of the passage.

Putting it into practice

Don't worry if you don't really understand how to apply this right now! On the next pages, I've given you some sample passages to look at to see how you might identify the key features of HoVerCrafT. Don't feel that you have to annotate the passages to this extent when you're practicing, I've just done it to show you everything you could find.

There are four sample passages here, which I've deliberately chosen to represent some of the most common layouts that you'll see on the ACT Scientific Reasoning. I haven't put questions in at this stage; we'll get to those later. There are two experiment passages, and two data representation passages. There's a blank one first, for you to try annotating and picking out key details. Then, there are my annotations so you can see whether you've missed anything important, and for you to consider whether you need to adapt your strategy.

Remember, this isn't a memory exercise! Think of annotating the passage as giving yourself a roadmap for what to look for when you're doing the questions. Locate the important information using HoVerCrafT so you can find it when you need to answer the questions.

Passage I

Rehydration solutions are solutions designed to replace fluids lost from blood plasma and extracellular fluid. They are needed to treat conditions involving dehydration, including diarrhea caused by intestinal pathogens. These diseases are a leading cause of death, especially among children in developing countries.

Intestinal absorption of water relies on osmosis – the process by which water moves from an area of low concentration to an area of high concentration across a membrane. In the small intestine, the Na^+/glucose symport protein (SGLT1) draws two sodium ions and one molecule of glucose across the epithelial cells lining the membrane. The glucose molecules and sodium ions are then transported into the bloodstream by another cellular mechanism. Each set of transported molecules is accompanied by many water molecules to maintain osmostic equilibrium. Hydration levels are measured by osmolality, which is the number of solvent particles per kilogram of solvent. Normal blood plasma osmolality is 280–295 mOsm/kg.

Experiments were conducted to determine the best osmolality for rehydration solutions.

Experiment 1

A 25 mL bag made of a semipermeable plastic containing a 15 mL sample of normally hydrated plasma was placed in a beaker. The beaker was filled with 50 mL of a rehydration solution. The solution was then observed for ten minutes, and the volume of the bag at the end was measured.

	Intial osmolality (mOsm/kg)	Osmolality of added solution	Final bag volume (mL)
Bag 1	285	310	20
Bag 2	285	300	17
Bag 3	275	310	19
Bag 4	275	300	18

Table 1

Experiment 2

A sample of intestinal tissue was fixed in a small container. The chamber on the left was filled with 50 mL of 275 mOsm/kg solution. The chamber on the right was filled with 50 mL of 300 mOsm/kg solution. A probe on the right measures the changing concentrations of Na^+ and glucose in the solution at 30-second intervals. The results are shown below:

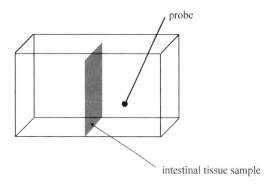

probe

intestinal tissue sample

Figure 1

Key:
····· Glucose
— Na^+

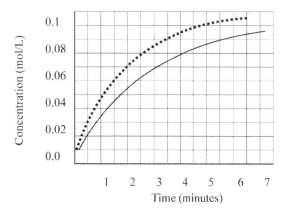

Figure 2

Passage I

Rehydration solutions are solutions designed to replace fluids lost from blood plasma and extracellular fluid. They are needed to treat conditions involving dehydration, including diarrhea caused by intestinal pathogens. These diseases are a leading cause of death, especially among children in developing countries.

explanation

Intestinal absorption of water relies on osmosis, the process by which water moves from an area of low concentration to an area of high concentration across a membrane. In the small intestine, the Na⁺/glucose symport protein (SGLT1) draws two sodium ions and one molecule of glucose across the epithelial cells lining the membrane. The glucose molecules and sodium ions are then transported into the bloodstream by another cellular mechanism. Each set of transported molecules is accompanied by many water molecules to maintain osmotic equilibrium. Hydration levels are measured by osmolality, which is the number of solvent particles per kilogram of solvent. Normal blood plasma osmolality is 280–295 mOsm/kg.

Experiments were conducted to determine the best osmolality for rehydration solutions.] H

Experiment 1

A 25 mL bag made of a semipermeable plastic containing a 15 mL sample of normally hydrated plasma was placed in a beaker. The beaker was filled with 50 mL of a rehydration solution. The solution was then observed for ten minutes, and the volume of the bag at the end was measured.

Y (I)   V (I)   V (D)

	Initial osmolality (mOsm/kg)	Osmolality of added solution	Final bag volume (mL)
Bag 1	285	310	20
Bag 2	285	300	17
Bag 3	275	310	19
Bag 4	275	300	18

original was 15 mL

Table 1

Experiment 2

A sample of intestinal tissue was fixed in a small container. The chamber on the left was filled with 50 mL of 275 mOsm/kg solution. The chamber on the right was filled with 50 mL of 300 mOsm/kg solution. A probe on the right measures the changing concentrations of Na⁺ and glucose in the solution at 30-second intervals. The results are shown below:

compare with Bag 4

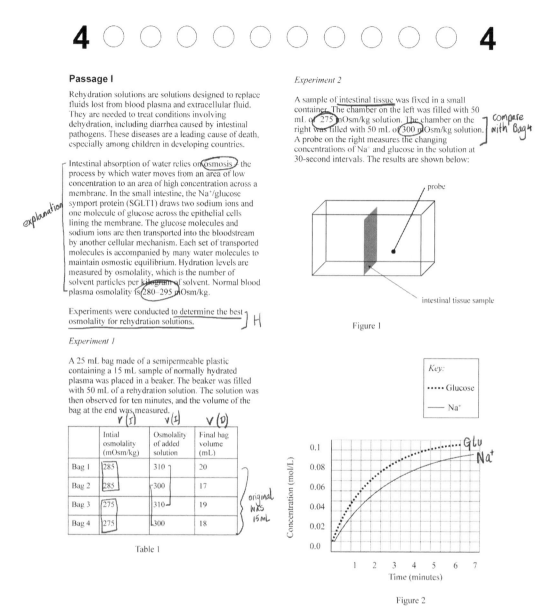

probe

intestinal tissue sample

Figure 1

Key:
····· Glucose
— Na⁺

Glu
Na⁺

Figure 2

This passage contains a lot of different types of data (tables, graphs and text), so it's important to identify where the information is located in the passage, and which parts can be matched with which other parts. In Table 1, you can see how the information is structured: Bags 1 and 2 have the same initial osmolality, as do Bags 3 and 4, whereas Bags 1 and 3 are comparable for the added solution, as are Bags 2 and 4. This type of data structure is quite common. It's also important to identify that the conditions in experiment 2 used the same set-up as Bag 4, so if you have to compare experiments 1 and 2, you'll need to refer to Bag 4 as your connection. There is a complicated explanation in the second paragraph of text. It's definitely not a good idea to read it, just remember that it's there. The most important parts of HoVerCrafT here are H and V.

Passage II

During an earthquake, ground water pressure in sand and silt soil areas increases rapidly, and the soil composition becomes more liquid — a process known as liquefaction. This often means that the soil is unable to support the weight of buildings that have foundations in the liquifacted areas.

Liquefaction also causes the ground to flatten, evening out peaks and troughs in the ground that buildings or other structures may be built upon.

In some regions, depending on soil composition, the liquefied soil will cause damping effects, meaning an earthquake's effects will be less severe. Other regions with different soil compositions will suffer from amplifying effects, meaning that the vibrations of the earthquake are more severe.

A series of measurements were recorded by sensors during a recent earthquake.

Figure 1 shows the soil composition over a 2 km region between points P and Q.

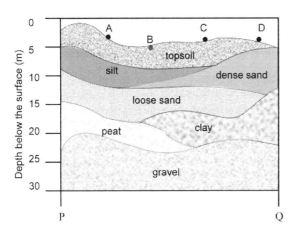

Figure 1

Study 1

The four sites in Figure 1 were measured during the earthquake. Figure 2 shows their change in position during the earthquake.

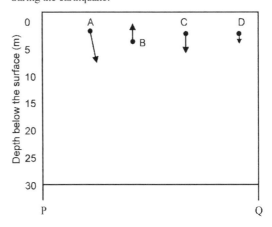

Figure 2

Study 2

In the region that suffered from the earthquake, many buildings were damaged. In order to rebuild effectively, data on the foundations of the original buildings in that area were collected and recorded in Table 1.

Number of storeys	Average foundation depth (m)	Soil composition surrounding foundations
1—3	3	topsoil, dense sand
3—15	10	topsoil, dense sand, silt
15—30	21	topsoil, dense sand, silt, loose sand, clay, peat
30+	43	all types

Table 1

4 ○ ○ ○ ○ ○ ○ ○ ○ ○ **4**

Passage II

During an earthquake, ground water pressure in sand and silt soil areas increases rapidly, and the soil composition becomes more liquid — a process known as liquefaction. This often means that the soil is unable to support the weight of buildings that have foundations in the liquifacted areas.

topic (H)

Liquefaction also causes the ground to flatten, evening out peaks and troughs in the ground that buildings or other structures may be built upon.

In some regions, depending on soil composition, the liquefied soil will cause damping effects, meaning an earthquake's effects will be less severe. Other regions with different soil compositions will suffer from amplifying effects, meaning that the vibrations of the earthquake are more severe.

effects

A series of measurements were recorded by sensors during a recent earthquake.

Figure 1 shows the soil composition over a 2 km region between points P and Q.

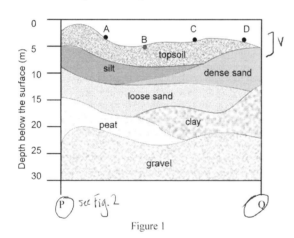

Figure 1

P) see fig. 2

Study 1

The four sites in Figure 1 were measured during the earthquake. Figure 2 shows their change in position during the earthquake.

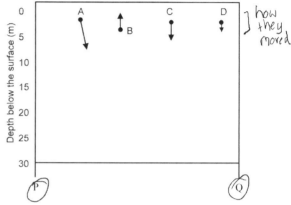

] how they moved

Figure 2

Study 2

In the region that suffered from the earthquake, many buildings were damaged. In order to rebuild effectively, data on the foundations of the original buildings in that area were collected and recorded in Table 1.

Number of storeys	Average foundation depth (m)	Soil composition surrounding foundations
1—3	3	topsoil, dense sand
3–15	10	topsoil, dense sand, silt
15–30	21	topsoil, dense sand, silt, loose sand, clay, peat
30+	43	all types

see Fig. 1

Table 1

This is a much simpler passage than the previous one. You can skim the text, as none of it is very complicated. You need to realize that Figures 1 and 2 have the same *x* axis, and therefore can be linked. Table 1 can also be linked to Figure 1 because they both talk about soil composition. That's pretty much it. In this passage, V is the only part of HoVerCrafT that you really need to pay attention to until you get to the questions.

4

Passage III

Some students conducted an experiment to test how the shape and weight of objects affected air resistance, in particular whether the shape of the object affected the turbulence of the air flow when the objects were falling through a wind tunnel. A fine white powder was diffused into the air so that the students could observe the flow of air past the object. Throughout their experiments, they noted whether the flow was laminar (flowing, distinct layers) or turbulent (random, chaotic air stream). They used the experimental set-up shown in Figure 1.

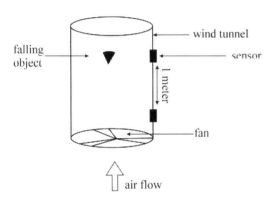

Figure 1

Experiment 1

The students took several different materials and cut a 10 cm × 10 cm square of each. They set the wind speed in the tunnel to 0.5 m/s and observed how long it took them to fall.

Material	Weight (g)	Time to fall 1 m (s)	Air flow
Paper*	1	21	turbulent
Card	3	18.5	turbulent
Copper	5	19.0	turbulent
Lead	10	18.0	turbulent
Aluminum	6	19.0	turbulent
Plastic	4	18.5	turbulent

* The paper was observed to bend in the wind tunnel.

Table 1

Experiment 2

The students constructed a set of cones from sheet aluminum. They varied the radius of each cone, keeping the height at 7 cm, and recorded the time taken to fall through the wind tunnel, using the procedure in Experiment 1.

Cone Radius (cm)	Weight (g)	Time to fall 1 m (s)	Air flow (l or t)
5	7	3.0	laminar
7	10	4.5	laminar
9	13	5.0	turbulent
11	15	5.5	turbulent
13	17	6.5	turbulent
15	18	7.5	turbulent

Experiment 3

The students constructed a further set of cones from sheet aluminum. They varied the height of each one, keeping the radius at 9 cm, and recorded the time taken to fall through the wind tunnel, using the procedure in Experiment 1.

Cone Height (cm)	Weight (g)	Time to fall 1 m (s)	Air flow (l or t)
3	7	3.0	turbulent
5	10	4.5	laminar
7	13	5.0	laminar
9	15	5.5	laminar

Passage III

Some students conducted an experiment to test how the shape and weight of objects affected air resistance, in particular whether the shape of the object affected the turbulence of the air flow when the objects were falling through a wind tunnel. A fine white powder was diffused into the air so that the students could observe the flow of air past the object. Throughout their experiments, they noted whether the flow was laminar (flowing, distinct layers) or turbulent (random, chaotic air stream). They used the experimental set-up shown in Figure 1.

H

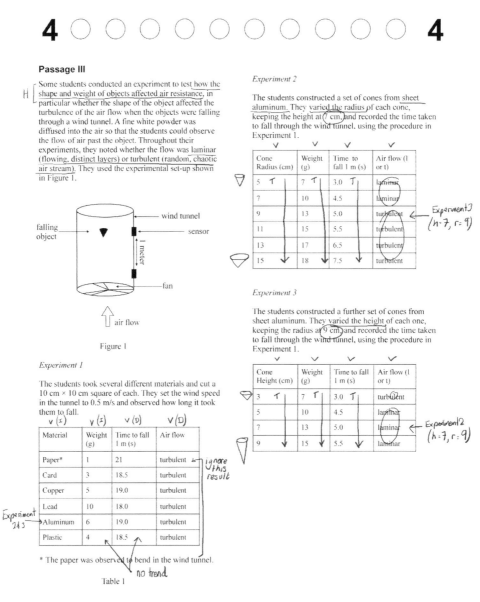

Figure 1

Experiment 1

The students took several different materials and cut a 10 cm × 10 cm square of each. They set the wind speed in the tunnel to 0.5 m/s and observed how long it took them to fall.

Material	Weight (g)	Time to fall 1 m (s)	Air flow
Paper*	1	21	turbulent
Card	3	18.5	turbulent
Copper	5	19.0	turbulent
Lead	10	18.0	turbulent
Aluminum	6	19.0	turbulent
Plastic	4	18.5	turbulent

* The paper was observed to bend in the wind tunnel.

Table 1

Experiment 2

The students constructed a set of cones from sheet aluminum. They varied the radius of each cone, keeping the height at 7 cm, and recorded the time taken to fall through the wind tunnel, using the procedure in Experiment 1.

Cone Radius (cm)	Weight (g)	Time to fall 1 m (s)	Air flow (l or t)
5	7	3.0	laminar
7	10	4.5	laminar
9	13	5.0	turbulent
11	15	5.5	turbulent
13	17	6.5	turbulent
15	18	7.5	turbulent

Experiment 3

The students constructed a further set of cones from sheet aluminum. They varied the height of each one, keeping the radius at 9 cm, and recorded the time taken to fall through the wind tunnel, using the procedure in Experiment 1.

Cone Height (cm)	Weight (g)	Time to fall 1 m (s)	Air flow (l or t)
3	7	3.0	turbulent
5	10	4.5	laminar
7	13	5.0	laminar
9	15	5.5	laminar

This is a great passage for HoVerCrafT! It's also a good one to test your visualization skills: try to picture what's happening in your head. From Table 1, you can conclude that weight and time to fall have no obvious trend. Also notice that if you need to cross reference between the three experiments, aluminum was used in all three, and the third rows in Tables 2 and 3 are actually the same cone (radius of 9 cm and height of 7 cm). One of my favorite strategies is using arrows to identify the trends (in Tables 2 and 3 you can see that I've drawn an arrow in the direction that the numbers are increasing). This is really helpful for answering questions, as you'll see later. The questions for this passage would likely focus on linking together this data, with perhaps one question about what can be concluded from the experiments or one that asks you about the design of the experiment.

Passage IV

Ice cores are long cylinders of compacted ice, formed by compression of snow over long periods of time. They are prepared by drilling down into ice (often from glaciers) and removing a vertical segment. Because ice cores form over long periods of time, they contain a preserved record of the climate, such as the composition of the air, and any airborne particles, such as soot, ash and dust, at the time that the layer was formed.

Volcanic eruptions can sometimes be dated from ice cores because they release solid particulates, such as dust and ash, as well as greenhouse gases such as CO_2, NO_2 and SO_2.

Researchers conducted two studies to determine whether a previously extracted ice core contained evidence of volcanic eruptions by comparing it to a more recent ice core that was formed during a period of high volcanic activity.

Study 1

The scientists extracted an ice core and used known meteorological data to add approximate dates, as shown in Figure 1. From this they were able to generate approximations of the greenhouse gas levels, as shown in Figure 2.

Study 2

Figure 3 shows climate measurements of greenhouse gas levels between 2001 and 2003. A dark band (shown on the graph) was observed in the ice core. Analysis of the composition of the dark band found it to be volcanic ash.

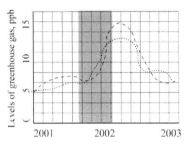

Figure 3

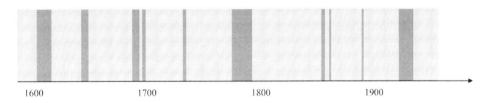

Figure 1

Figure 2

Passage IV

Ice cores are long cylinders of compacted ice, formed by compression of snow over long periods of time. They are prepared by drilling down into ice (often from glaciers) and removing a vertical segment. Because ice cores form over long periods of time, they contain a preserved record of the climate, such as the composition of the air, and any airborne particles, such as soot, ash and dust, at the time that the layer was formed.

possible H/C?

Volcanic eruptions can sometimes be dated from ice cores because they release solid particulates, such as dust and ash, as well as greenhouse gases such as CO_2, NO_2 and SO_2.

H

Researchers conducted two studies to determine whether a previously extracted ice core contained evidence of volcanic eruptions by comparing it to a more recent ice core that was formed during a period of high volcanic activity.

Study 2

Figure 3 shows climate measurements of greenhouse gas levels between 2001 and 2003. A dark band (shown on the graph) was observed in the ice core. Analysis of the composition of the dark band found it to be volcanic ash.

Study 1

The scientists extracted an ice core and used known meteorological data to add approximate dates, as shown in Figure 1. From this they were able to generate approximations of the greenhouse gas levels, as shown in Figure 2.

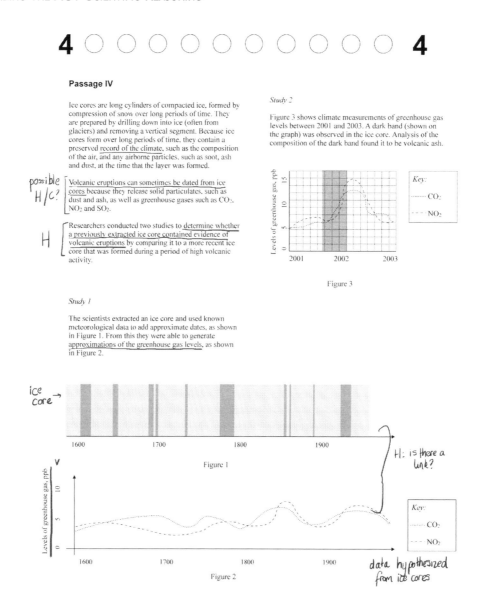

ice core →

Figure 1

H: is there a link?

Figure 2

data hypothesized from ice cores

This passage is on the simpler side, too. The most important parts of HoVerCrafT are the hypothesis and conclusions here. In the second and third paragraphs, the hypothesis is put forward that past levels of atmospheric gases can be measured indirectly by using ice cores. There is also a link with volcanic eruptions, as these affect levels of atmospheric gases, and can be seen in ice cores. Study 2 gives strength to this argument by using modern climate data and comparing it to data from an ice core. Study 1 makes a conclusion from the stated hypothesis (it deduces values of the greenhouse gases from the ice core measurements). The only variable here is the gas levels, but it's really important to understand the reasoning behind this passage. The questions for this type of passage would probably be more about reasoning than reading data.

Now that you've read through the passages and seen my annotations, you'll have some idea of what's important to notice about the passage. A really important thing to remember here is that HoVerCrafT helps you list all the things you could notice, but not all four would be in every passage. Make sure you're flexible with this strategy, and don't waste time trying to find all four points – they're not always there, and sometimes they're not important! Also remember that what you take in from your initial reading of the passage will likely change with time and experience, so don't worry if you don't feel very confident right now. Don't worry if your strategy ends up deviating a little from HoVerCrafT too – in my opinion, HoVerCrafT is the best starting point, but there's lots of possible variations.

Adapting HoVerCrafT for conflicting viewpoints passages

The "conflicting viewpoints" passages are mostly text based, and usually have seven questions. This makes them important – they have more questions per passage than any other. Your time investment in reading that passage has a great payoff because there are seven questions that can be answered from what you've read (versus only five or six questions from the other types of passage).

Beware! Some people recommend that you should do this passage last, with a surprising degree of certainty ... I think you should do what works for you. For some people, this is a difficult passage because there are lots of different ideas, and you need to read the text more thoroughly. Other people find it easy because it's more like the reading section. If you find the reading section is one of your better sections, then it may be that you like this passage. If you are a slow reader and usually need to skim the reading passage for key facts rather than reading in full, this may be one of the harder passages for you. The important thing is to try some tests and then decide what works for you. If you want to do it first, that's fine, if you want to do it last, that's fine too. Just don't get superstitious about it. In my experience, it doesn't matter that much. Focus on getting the questions right!

In the conflicting viewpoints passage, two or more people are discussing their ideas about the cause of something, or the best way of testing something. A common pitfall with these passages is to assume that the viewpoints are completely opposed to each other – they are not. Usually they agree on some points and disagree on others.

Sometimes the viewpoints are those of students, in which case some of them are wrong. For example, they conflict with ideas about science that you know, such as that burning requires oxygen. Be careful here though! You are supposed to **answer the questions according to the passage**, not according to what you know, unless the question says otherwise.

Most of the questions ask you whether each person would agree with a given statement, or which argument would be supported by a given piece of additional information. Remember that you need to read this type of passage more carefully – treat it like part of the reading comprehension section.

How to use HoVerCrafT

H: The hypothesis will probably be somewhere in the introductory paragraph, although it may not be stated as a hypothesis. If you can find a hypothesis, underline it. If not, note down the topic or main question of discussion.

V/T: Usually there are no tables in this section, so trends aren't relevant here. Since there aren't experiments either, variables aren't as relevant.

C: Because there's no experiment, you usually just have a series of conclusions. Note down each person's conclusion, or underline a sentence that encapsulates it. Some helpful points:

- When you're asked whether Researcher 1 would agree with Researcher 2 about a certain statement, refer back to their "conclusion" sentence that you found.

- Remember that you're never asked to decide who is correct. Sometimes you might know that some of the viewpoints are wrong, but don't choose an answer based on whether or not it is correct. Just focus on whether or not the viewpoints agree with the statement in the question.

As with the previous few pages, I've given you an example of a passage and how I would look at it. There's a blank one first for you to try, then one with my annotations so you can see whether you missed anything important.

4 ○ ○ ○ ○ ○ ○ ○ ○

Passage V

Telomeres are segments of nucleotides at the end of DNA. They consist of several repeated TTAGGG sequences. These signal the end of the DNA strand to the cellular machinery. Because the mechanisms for copying DNA to make new cells do not allow replication of the entire DNA strand all the way to the ends, some of the telomeres are lost with every replication. Telomeres can also be regenerated in some cells by telomerase reverse transcriptase. The function of telomeres is a current area of research, but it is thought that they play a role in cellular aging and control the number of times a given cell can replicate. Two scientists discuss the role of telomeres.

Scientist 1

Telomeres are primarily a protective mechanism for the DNA. One of their properties is the ability to absorb oxidative stress caused by free radical molecules. This prevents the oxidative stress impacting or altering the genetic material contained in the DNA. In this way, they protect the DNA from external damange. In cancerous cells, telomeres are found to be shortened or damaged, leading to chromosome damage and genetic mutations. Telomeres themselves are protected against damage by a group of proteins, which shows their importance as a cellular protective mechanism.

Scientist 2

The primary function of telomeres is not protection against cellular ageing, because they can be regenerated under some circumstances. If there was cellular damage and the telomerase reverse transcriptase repaired the telomeres then the cell would be able to replicate, thus telomeres would not be protecting the cell. In some species, telomeres can lengthen with age, rather than shorten, which indicates that their function is not simply protective. Further, some studies show that lifestyle factors alter the telomere length, for example sedentary behavior can decrease telomere length, while exercise can increase it. Therefore, telomeres are a molecular indicator of the overall health of the cell.

4 ◯ ◯ ◯ ◯ ◯ ◯ ◯ ◯ ◯ **4**

Passage V

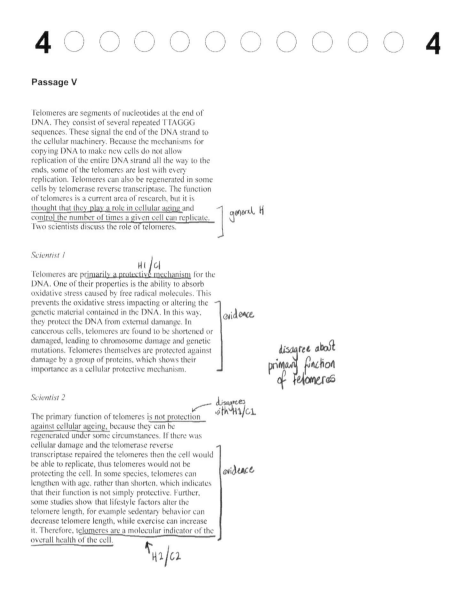

Telomeres are segments of nucleotides at the end of DNA. They consist of several repeated TTAGGG sequences. These signal the end of the DNA strand to the cellular machinery. Because the mechanisms for copying DNA to make new cells do not allow replication of the entire DNA strand all the way to the ends, some of the telomeres are lost with every replication. Telomeres can also be regenerated in some cells by telomerase reverse transcriptase. The function of telomeres is a current area of research, but it is thought that they play a role in cellular aging and control the number of times a given cell can replicate. Two scientists discuss the role of telomeres.

general H

Scientist 1

H1 / C1

Telomeres are primarily a protective mechanism for the DNA. One of their properties is the ability to absorb oxidative stress caused by free radical molecules. This prevents the oxidative stress impacting or altering the genetic material contained in the DNA. In this way, they protect the DNA from external damage. In cancerous cells, telomeres are found to be shortened or damaged, leading to chromosome damage and genetic mutations. Telomeres themselves are protected against damage by a group of proteins, which shows their importance as a cellular protective mechanism.

evidence

disagree about primary function of telomeres

Scientist 2

disagrees with H1/C1

The primary function of telomeres is not protection against cellular ageing, because they can be regenerated under some circumstances. If there was cellular damage and the telomerase reverse transcriptase repaired the telomeres then the cell would be able to replicate, thus telomeres would not be protecting the cell. In some species, telomeres can lengthen with age, rather than shorten, which indicates that their function is not simply protective. Further, some studies show that lifestyle factors alter the telomere length, for example sedentary behavior can decrease telomere length, while exercise can increase it. Therefore, telomeres are a molecular indicator of the overall health of the cell.

evidence

↑ H2/C2

This is a nice one, because you might have studied telomeres in school. If so, you'll find this easier, and can probably skip the first paragraph entirely. If not, don't worry. Skim the first paragraph to get a brief idea of what telomeres do (the summary sentence I would have in my head is: "Telomeres are at the ends of DNA and they might be to do with aging and protection of DNA"). There's a general hypothesis stated in the first paragraph. It's vital that you identify the points of view of the two scientists. For Scientist 1, it's in the first sentence, whereas for Scientist 2, it's the last sentence. Notice that they are not directly disagreeing with each other, but they disagree about the **primary** function of telomeres.

Remember that with conflicting viewpoints, you need to read more thoroughly than the other passages, but if you're struggling to understand the passage, it's OK to just identify the information as I have by labelling H or C, and evidence, as I have above.

Understanding graphs, charts, tables and diagrams

Graphs, charts and tables are your friend on the ACT! They're great because without them, the information would be presented in a sentence, which is so much harder. Consider this:

When the pressure was 6 kPa, the temperature was 278 K, but when the pressure was increased to 8 kPa, the temperature rose to 299 K. Then when the pressure dropped to 4 kPa, the temperature dropped to 257 K. This all happened in a 5 L container, but when we did the same experiment using a 2 L container, the pressure at 6 kPa was 357 K for the same volume of gas, dropping to 321 K for 4 kPa and rising to 401 K when the pressure was 8 kPa.

vs. this:

5 L container		2 L container	
Pressure (kPa)	Temperature (K)	Pressure (kPa)	Temperature (K)
4	257	4	321
6	278	6	357
8	299	8	401

What a mess! See how much nicer the table is! There's a very good reason why the table is easier to read than the text. The information in the table is presented so that you can navigate it. When you read the sentence, you get lost in all the numbers. When you read the tables, you know immediately what information you're being presented with, because of the layout. You know that there were two different situations (because the table is in two parts), and you know that each measured the same two variables (temperature and pressure) against each other. You don't even need to read the numbers!

Your key to success on the ACT scientific reasoning is to use this to your advantage. **Use the headings and labels to navigate yourself around the passage.**

Hopefully you've already figured out that this is the smartest approach to take, because it's really an application of the V and T parts of HoVerCrafT. You identify the V (variables) just by looking at the headings of the table, and you identify the T (trends) by looking at the pattern in the numbers.

Dependent and independent variables

Variables come in two kinds! Dependent variables are the ones you are investigating, whereas independent ones are the ones that you change. For example, if you change a concentration and investigate the effect this has on the rate of reaction, concentration is your independent variable and rate of reaction is your dependent variable. This is because you changed the concentration and measured the resulting rate of reaction. It usually makes the most sense to think of the **independent variable as the change** and the **dependent variable as the result**.

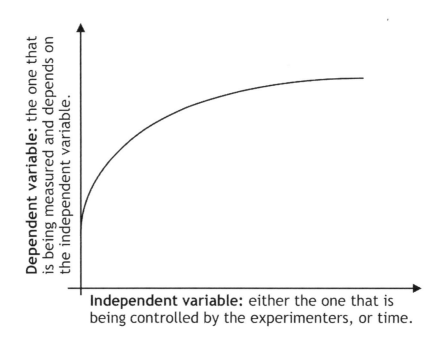

This might also help you to remember that in a graph, dependent variables go on the *y* axis (because they are the result) and independent variables go on the *x* axis (they are the input of your experiment). If one of your variables is time, it will always be the independent variable – not that you're changing time (because you can't!), but you're investigating a behavior that depends on time. Be careful though, if you are measuring a rate, such as in the example above, that could be the independent variable. Rate is not the same as time. It's also worth noting that in a data representation passage, you might not have dependent and independent variables, just ones that are linked. This means that there's a relationship, but it's not known whether A is causing B, or the other way around. The rule is that if your experiment has a dependent variable, it must go on the *y* axis, but just because something is on the *y* axis does not make it dependent on the variable that's on the *x* axis. Read that sentence over again to check that you understand. There are some graph examples on the next page to help you out.

Another important part of experiment design, and one that the ACT Scientific Reasoning tests quite frequently, is your knowledge of controls. Controls are what make your experiment valid! For example, if you are measuring the growth of plants in a shady spot versus a sunny spot, you want to make sure that the soil and rainfall are the same in both places (i.e. soil and rain are your controls). Otherwise, your observations might actually be caused by rainfall differences, but you would wrongly attribute them to differences in sunlight levels.

Quantitative and qualitative variables

There are two further ways that we can classify types of variables. If the variable has a numerical value (length, time, mass, concentration), then it's quantitative, or numerical. If it is a description (a month, a type or category, a color), then it's qualitative.

Continuous and discrete data

Continuous data can take any value. For example, a length could be 2 m, 2.05 m or 2.005 m. The limit is only in the way you're measuring. But shoe size can only be certain values. There is no such thing as a size 8.75. Numerical data can be continuous or discrete, but qualitative data can only be discrete – you always have to specify categories. Yes, there are an infinite number of eye colors, but if you're recording eye color, you will choose categories like "blue," "green" and "blue-green." You probably won't have "green with a tiny hint of blue" and "green with a miniscule hint of blue" – and even if you did, you still have a finite number of categories!

The method of presenting the data is dictated by what kind of data it is. Here are some samples so you can understand what kind of data you're looking at when you see a graph. My apologies to ornithology experts I might have offended by completely making up this data!

A bar graph displays one numerical data set (number of nests) against different categories (types of bird)

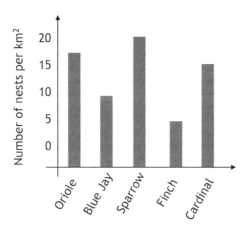

Bar graphs can also have divided bars so that they can convey an extra piece of information, like this one, which shows the number of nests in different regions, but also the different types of birds in these nests.

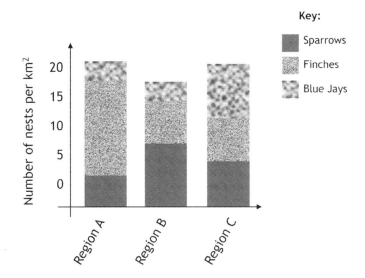

Information that's in bar graphs could also be presented in a table. A bar graph that has divided bars would become a divided table, like this one.

	Region A			Region B		
	Finches	Sparrows	Orioles	Finches	Sparrows	Orioles
2008	4	8	2	4	6	3
2009	5	4	7	9	6	2
2010	7	7	3	10	4	9
2011	10	4	8	3	6	12

A line graph shows a trend, such as a change in a certain quantity over time. Line graphs can incorporate extra data sets by having more than one line on the same graph.

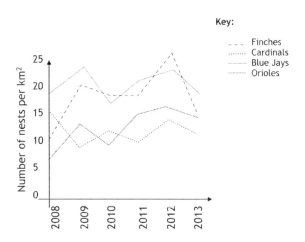

A scatter graph shows a numerical relationship between two variables.

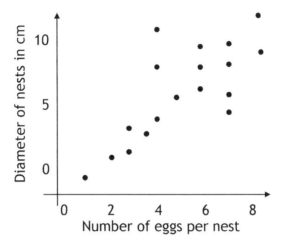

A circle graph (also known as a pie chart) shows a proportion visually; it shows how much of the total is made up of this specific part.

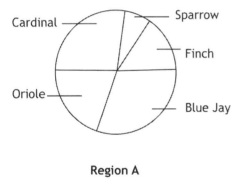

Region A

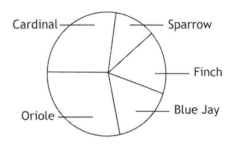

Region B

A frequency chart shows you how often something occurs, or how common it is. In this chart, the most common number of eggs to be found was 3. The least common was 7. Sometimes the y axis is a percentage – other times it is a proportion of the total.

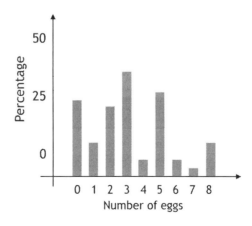

What's the difference between a line graph and a scatter plot?

Sometimes very little. Scatter plots show discrete data points, whereas line graphs show a continuous trend. For example, in the line graph above, it's reasonable to assume that half-way through 2010, there were about 1500 sparrows, because that value is in the middle of two existing data points. Technically, the number of sparrows is a discrete value, because half a sparrow is not a sparrow, but we're talking about such large numbers and we're approximating the number of sparrows anyway, so it's pretty much OK to read between the data points.

Consider the scatter graph above though. If you read between two data points, you might conclude that a nest with a 0.5 m diameter will contain 7.5 eggs. That's clearly silly! This data is discrete, and it's neither an approximation, nor a very large number, so it's not appropriate to read between two data points. Hence, this data is displayed as discrete values, not as a trend.

So what kinds of charts and graphs actually appear on the ACT?

Luckily for you, I went through every past paper published between 2007 and 2016 to come up with this list. That's almost 200 ACT Scientific Reasoning passages! Most passages use more than one chart or graph, but here's how many of each kind appear in those 200 passages.

Data type	Frequency	Where to find one in this book
Bar chart/histogram	29	Page 23
Table	99	right here!
Line graph	101	Page 24
Experimental set-up	49	Page 13
Cross section	5	Page 52
Map	2	I think you know what a map is!
Cross section graph	5	Page 11
Chemical equation	8	Page 47
Mathematical formula	10	Page 75
Biological diagram	12	Page 52
Karyotype	1	Page 56
Electric circuit	4	Page 64
Dichotomous key	1	Page 54
Flowchart	3	
Part of periodic table	1	Page 44
Pie chart/circle graph	1	Page 25

Some other graph weirdness you might see

Some graphs have two y axes! This might be surprising, but it happens in one of two situations:

1. You are plotting two different pieces of data whose trends you want to compare, but they have a different scale. For example, in this graph, rainfall and temperature have different units of measurement, but it is useful to see a connected trend.

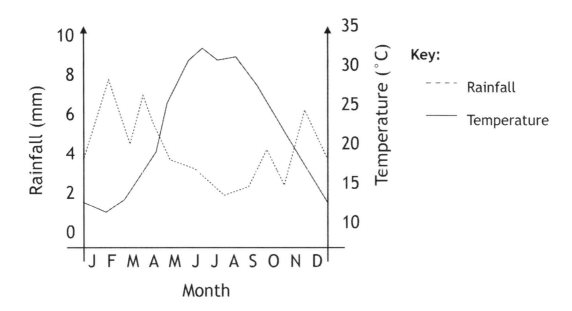

2. You are showing two different pieces of data that are both dependent on the same thing. For example, in this graph, both company A and company B are in the same industry, but company A is a smaller company.

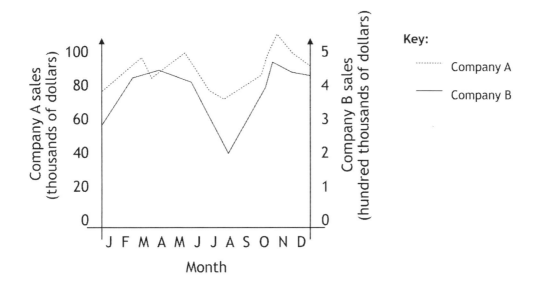

Sometimes a graph has the opposite units to what you're asked about in the question. This isn't really a weird graph, more that the graph has the opposite units to the question. The most common example of this is absorbance and reflectance of light. Those are opposite, that is, if 40% of the light is absorbed, 60% is reflected. So if the graph is showing absorbance, and the question asks for reflectance, subtract from 100 to get the other percentage.

Some graphs are divided into regions. A common example of this is a phase diagram. Each substance has its own specific phase diagram, which shows whether it's a solid, liquid or gas (or a different state, such as plasma) at a certain temperature and pressure. The axis on the graph will be temperature and pressure – usually pressure on the y axis, but there's no good reason for this. Depending on the combination of temperature and pressure, the substance will be in a different state.

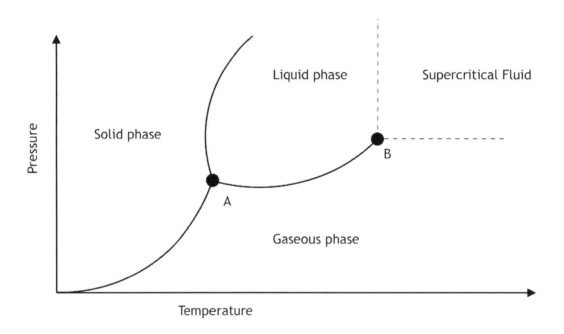

In this diagram, you can see that at low pressure and low temperature, a substance will be in the solid phase. As you increase the temperature (still at low pressure), the substance will cross into the gaseous phase. When a substance changes directly from solid phase to gas phase, this is known as sublimation.

Point A is known as the triple point. At exactly this pressure and temperature, the solid, liquid and gas phases of the substance coexist. Point B is the critical point, where the substance exists simultaneously as a liquid and a gas. Increasing the temperature or pressure from the critical point results in a supercritical fluid. Supercritical fluids are a bit weird – I suggest you find some videos of them so you can see them for real.

Tools for working with graphs

Here are the main things that you have to do when confronted with a graph on the ACT Scientific Reasoning.

1. **Reading the graph.** Some questions are simply just reading data from a graph. Look for wording such as, "when x is a, what is y?" These questions can become more complicated when more than two quantities are referred to, such as, "in Experiment 3, when measuring the change in p, when q was 40, what was s?" Be sure that you are looking at the right pieces of data! It's very helpful to put your finger on the information that you're using, so if the question says "according to Figure 1," place your finger on Figure 1 as you read.

2. **Extrapolation and interpolation.** Extrapolating is when you guess a value that's outside the range of your data by extending a trend. Interpolating is doing the same thing, but guessing a value within your data set (i.e. reading between two points). You are required to do this from graphs and tables.

3. **Identify how two variables relate to each other.** These questions typically have answers that are phrased as, "when x increases, y decreases" or other combinations. Make sure you read these choices carefully and select the right one – it's very easy to choose the wrong one by accident here, as the words in the answers are so similar! I've got some good tactics for this type of question on page 34. If you're looking at a graph to answer this question, look for correlation – is it positive (an increase-increase relationship like the graph on the left), or is it negative (an increase-decrease relationship, like the middle graph)? Remember that it could also be zero correlation (right-hand graph).

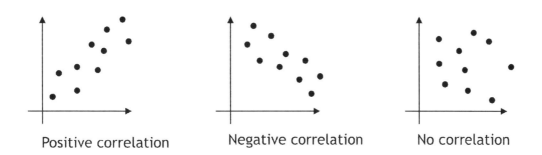

Positive correlation   Negative correlation   No correlation

If you're looking at a table, draw arrows in the direction that the numbers are increasing. If the arrows go the same way, it's an increase-increase relationship. You'll remember that I suggested this in my annotated examples for using HoVerCrafT.

4. This is the hardest type of graph-based question. You have to match two or three pieces of information between different graphs. Your key to answering this type of question correctly is to **use the labels of the axes and headings of the tables to navigate**. Work out where one piece of data would fit into another graph by matching up the labels on the axes. It's hard to be specific about these questions, because they come in all sorts of shapes and sizes. You might recognize them when you are reading the question and find yourself thinking, "I don't know where to start!"

Question types

So what types of questions am I actually answering?

If all you've done for the Scientific Reasoning section is followed this book, then you haven't seen any real questions yet! That's OK – by this point, you're already set up with the approach you need.

Approximately 30 questions ask you to read one or two pieces of data and connect them in some way. For example, you may have to:

1. Identify a single piece of data.

2. Draw a conclusion from two pieces of data together (applying the ideas of one experiment to the other).

3. Identify trends in the data, extrapolate or interpolate.

4. Suggest a reason or cause from a piece of information, which often involves you reasoning about the hypothesis of the experiment, or proposing an appropriate conclusion.

Around five questions ask you to:

5. Identify the variable or state why the experiment was designed a certain way, including the experimental controls.

About five questions ask you to:

6. Visualize an experimental set-up (e.g. moving parts in a physics experiment, or bacteria growth in a biology experiment).

7. Provide reasons from your own knowledge.

8. Connect trends in a mathematical way, or use a formula.

Points 1 and 2 are usually quite easy. The HoVerCrafT strategy has you covered on points 3 and 5. Point 4 comes with practice, but it's very much related to HoVerCrafT and your general understanding of the passage. We've talked about 6, but it might take you a little practice to get it right. Points 7 and 8 are covered in the knowledge section.

I deliberately haven't given examples of these types of question here because you're just about to see them for real on a test, and I also think it's much better to learn from specific ACT designed questions. The ACT is a large organization that designs its tests very carefully according to certain standards and formulas. Naturally, I don't know these, because I don't work for the ACT! Many tests designed by other organizations don't accurately prepare you for the ACT because their questions aren't realistic. There are some books and programs that do have realistic questions, so read some reviews before you buy   they're not all bad.

Instead, I've guided you to where you can find five real past tests that the ACT has published, and I've given answer explanations for these at the end of the book. I've also given an index to the question types and where you can find each of the above types in each of the five tests. You should use this to see if you are consistently making the same types of errors. It's very important that you use the answer explanations for any questions you got wrong once you've done the test. A test on which you've analyzed your mistakes is worth about five that you've completed without analyzing! I'm going to repeat this advice later on, too, because it's so important!

How to take a practice test

First, you should practice from official ACT papers where possible, as I've said. The ACT has published five past tests online, so start with those. You can either find them yourself, or visit prepACTSAT.com/ACT-official-tests to find links to the ones from the ACT website (they are also on the ACT website, but hard to find!).

You absolutely must print these tests out! The real test is on paper, and reading from paper is very different to reading from a screen. If you would like to save paper and you have good eyesight, print two pages per sheet.

For your first few tests, take as much time as you need: don't rush, but don't spend ages working on a single question (you want this to be reflective of how you would perform on the test for real). Use HoVerCrafT for every passage. After you've got used to the test and timing, you can aim to finish in 35 minutes. Here are my test instructions:

- Set aside 50 minutes in a quiet space where you know you won't be interrupted. Make a "do not disturb" sign if you have to!

- Find a stopwatch to time yourself. If you have to use your phone to time yourself, put it in airplane mode so nothing distracts you.

- Don't use a bubble sheet (answer sheet) initially, just circle the answers on the test paper. After you've got used to the test, use the answer sheet as well (I talk about how to fill this out later on page 80).

- Set a timer for 35 minutes and begin the test.

- When the timer sounds, write "35 mins" by the question you're on, and draw a line under it.

- Now set a stopwatch to count how much time you take to finish the test. When you mark the test, include these questions, too.

Absolutely ALWAYS take up the test. Mark it and go over your mistakes. If you do not learn from your mistakes you will repeat them, so save yourself effort and mark your test conscientiously. I'll keep emphasizing this point: it's the most important factor in effective test prep.

A tutor's top six tips

1. The most common mistake on ACT Scientific Reasoning

Other than just not understanding either the passage or the question, most mistakes on this section happen when you are **looking at the wrong thing**. I know it sounds so obvious, but I wouldn't be pointing this out if I hadn't said it many times to my students!

It's all too easy to look at the wrong line on a graph (e.g. reading from the solid line instead of the dashed line), getting a trend question wrong because you say two quantities increase together when you mean that as one increases, the other decreases. It's also very easy to look for 0.02 on a scale when you mean 0.2. I'm writing this because it once caused me to get stuck for about five minutes! Lastly, make sure you are looking at the right experiment. If it says experiment 1, make sure you really are looking at experiment 1. I know this is so obvious, but remember that you are under time pressure.

2. How to look at the test after you've done it

I call this "taking up the test." You need to **look at every mistake you made**, and it's a good idea to look at any answer you were unsure of, too. Circle the correct answer, and then work out why you made the mistake. I have answer explanations for the five official ACT practice tests, which are available online for free, so you can use these to help you out. They start on page 113.

It's helpful to actually make a list of reasons for your errors. Possible reasons include: "I was rushing," "I looked at the wrong table," "I didn't read the questions carefully," "I didn't understand which pieces of data to use in answering the question," etc. Try to be as specific as possible. If you need an example, look at "a tally chart of 'why I made my mistakes'" in the Useful Things appendix. When you have finished, you'll be able to see clearly what you should do differently next time. This will be even more applicable once you start doing these tests under timed conditions.

This might be tedious, but it will save you time. Looking at your past tests in detail is essential to improving. If you don't take up your tests and look at why you made mistakes, you're not actually learning. This means that your prep will consist of endless repetition, which is even more boring than analyzing your mistakes! In my opinion, one test that has been completed in one sitting and taken up properly is worth about five that have been written without taking them up. This fits in well with my motto: **work smart not hard**! The most successful students are the ones who work out exactly what mistakes they are making, and avoid them the next time around. This requires dedication and focus, but it's a great learning habit to develop.

3. Fill in the bubble sheet right!

Depending on how you approach tests, you may not use a bubble sheet that much. At a minimum, you should have used the actual ACT answer sheet on two practice tests, under timed conditions, before test day. If you are someone who is prone to getting stressed out on test day, or you are very tight for time after practicing this section several times, you should use it more often. There's one at the end of every official ACT practice test that is just like the real thing.

The most efficient way to fill in the bubble sheet is after every passage. This way, you don't have to think about it when you're actually answering the questions, but you're not leaving it until the end of the test either. It means you won't run out of time filling it in at the end of the test, and you won't waste time by finding your place on it throughout the test. It also functions as a mental break between passages.

I've actually used my students as guinea pigs here and tested various ways of filling in the bubble sheet. I'm convinced that this is the best, so you should use it for the other sections, too.

4. Have a guess letter!

Some people get weirdly hung up about guessing and think that they should do a pattern on the bubble sheet or not choose the same letter over again or something else bizarre. THIS IS NOT TRUE! All letters are equally likely and there is no way to "guess better." **Choose your guess letter right now, and use it for all the tests.** This means you won't waste time worrying on test day about which letter or pattern to fill in. You have a quarter chance of getting the right answer for each question, and it's as simple as that. Anyone who says anything different is playing mind games with you, and encouraging you to waste valuable test time!

5. Know when process of elimination is good

Process of elimination (crossing out answers that you know are wrong) shouldn't usually be the first thing you do. It's quite time consuming to read all the choices and consider each one, but if you can't understand the passage or the question, then **process of elimination is a great second strategy.** This applies to all the other sections on the test too! Sometimes people say that multiple choice is easier because you have the answer in front of you. That depends on how you use the answers. If you waste time considering every single option on every single question, you're making multiple choice harder!

6. Know when to answer questions with answers like this:

- A. Yes, because [reason 1]
- B. Yes, because [reason 2]
- C. No, because [reason 1]
- D. No, because [reason 2]

You have two ways to approach this question, which is useful, because often these questions are very wordy. You can **start by deciding whether reason 1 or reason 2 is true**, which will eliminate two choices either way. This helps a lot, because the second part is much harder to decide. Working out the best reason is simply a case of fact checking in the passage, whereas deciding whether to choose yes or no requires you to really understand the passage, which you may not.

Thanks for staying with me this far! Now you're ready to look more closely at timing.

The Timing

Diagnose yourself

We're going to do a timing exercise to begin, which will help you to understand what you need to work on. Based on your results, you'll follow one of two suggested study programs, which I've called Path 1 and Path 2. If you're going through this book in order (and I suggest that you do), you'll have just done a test. You can use that one as Test 1 in this exercise, but to make sure that you're getting a representative sample, you need to do another test under the same conditions. Just in case you need a reminder, we are using official ACT practice tests, and you are not aiming to complete them in 35 minutes. Read the instructions on page 31 if you need a reminder. Record your start and end time, and take a reasonable amount of time – as much as you need, but don't spend ages working on a single question! Ideally, your time shouldn't exceed 50 minutes.

Before you go any further, ensure you've "taken up the test." If you can't remember what I mean by that, check back to page 33 (number 2). This is a VITAL step in your prep, so don't skip it!

Most students struggle to finish the ACT Scientific Reasoning section first time around in 35 minutes. This is normal. Now you have learned how to focus on the right information using HoVer-CrafT you'll be a little quicker. Your main strategy for finishing the test on time is to practice! In my experience, about 50% of students find that practice alone is enough to ensure that they finish the test. By the time they do the Scientific Reasoning section for the third or fourth time, they're familiar enough with it to be able to hone in on the relevant information and finish the test, possibly with time left to check it over.

It's important to mention here that some tests only have six passages, not the usual seven. Treat this as a bonus if it happens, but don't assume it will.

Now that you've taken up the two tests, fill in this table:

	Questions completed in 35 minutes	Amount of extra time needed	Raw score	Scaled score	Target score
Test 1			/40	/36	/36
Test 2			/40	/36	/36

For the last box, you will need to know roughly what score range you are aiming for. This will depend on what schools you want to apply to. Take the average ACT score for the schools you want to apply for. If you don't know this yet, check out the Useful Things appendix. Alternatively, if you've already done a test, take your highest section score as your science target (e.g. if you took a practice test and scored 27 on English, 28 on Math, 23 on Reading and 21 on Scientific Reasoning, make your target science score a 28 out of 36). If you haven't done anything except what's in this book yet, and you have no idea where you want to go to school, just add 4 to the score you just got.

Now look at the following two tables and choose Path 1 or Path 2. I'm assuming here that you've done the science section in full less than twice. If you've already done more than five Scientific Reasoning sections, and you're still looking to improve, choose the Path 2 regardless. If your scores were quite different on the two tests in the table above, you can choose to take the average of your tests, or the one you feel is most reflective of your performance. Be honest with yourself.

I split my advice into two Paths here because most students make quite a big initial improvement over their first five practice tests, just because they get used to the questions, structure and wording. Most of the timing strategies I discuss in Path 2 involve some compromise, and so if you're likely to be able to improve to where you need to be just through practice, you should follow Path 1.

Path 1:

Questions completed in 35 minutes	Amount of extra time needed	Raw score	Gap between scaled and target score
32 or more	6 minutes or less	32 or more /40	5 points or fewer

Path 2:

Questions completed in 35 minutes	Amount of extra time needed	Raw Score	Gap between scaled and target score
Fewer than 32	More than 6 minutes	Fewer than 32/40	5 points or more

Path 1

Path 1 students:

- Feel as if they usually understand more than four of the passages on the test

- Feel pretty confident answering most of the questions

- Usually don't feel rushed on the test

- Want to improve by fewer than five points

If this is you, in all likelihood you just need more practice. Do one more practice test under the same conditions as you did above, go over all of your mistakes, and see if you improve. If you knocked off more than two minutes, or your score improved by more than one point, that's great, you're probably on the right path.

What do you need to do now?

- Most importantly, keep practicing. The most important advice for you in this whole book is to **take up your tests**. If you do this consistently, you can almost certainly make that five-point improvement.

- Look over the timing strategies in Path 2 anyway. You never know what might be helpful, but do remember that most of them are compromises that may end up hurting your score.

- Make sure you check out the knowledge sections later on to brush up.

- From now until you first intend to write the ACT, do one science practice section per week.

- Also check out the Useful Things appendix.

Path 2

Path 2 students:

- Don't feel ready to write the Scientific Reasoning section of the test yet for real

- Often feel rushed when they're writing the test

- Feel like they don't understand most of the passages on the test

- Need to improve by more than five points

If this is you, you're going to need to put in some work. That's not a bad thing, and despite what some people say about how useless and subjective these tests are, I do believe that the data-based reasoning skills that this section tests are valuable. You will probably never be asked to do a test that's exactly like this again, but in practicing, you are developing a skill that will be valuable in other ways, although you might not notice it. If you're committed to improving your score, you can. Don't be discouraged if it's not what you want initially. Most students can improve their score by 2-5 points with good advice and dedicated practice. I have seen students improve their scores on this section by more than ten points, although it's not easy to do! There is something I'd like to warn you about though.

Tests aren't everything. This is one section of a test that forms one part of your application. Different schools view tests differently, and they may also not attach much importance to the Scientific Reasoning section. No one can tell you exactly how much this section matters to your application, because that depends on all the other parts of your application, which likely say a lot more about you as a person than your score on this test section. But be aware of this. Don't be losing sleep over the ACT Scientific Reasoning. After a certain point, your efforts are better spent on activities that benefit both you and your application - make sure your application shows how you excel at something you're passionate about, not just that you have a great test score. The point at which you decide to focus your efforts away from the ACT is for you to decide, but make sure you remember that there is a time and a place to do that.

What do you need to do now?

- Most importantly, keep practicing, keep taking up your tests, and keep applying HoVer-CrafT.

- Read the timing strategies on the next page.

- Follow the rest of this book as thoroughly as you can.

- From now until you first intend to write the ACT, do at least one practice section per week.

Timing strategies

Here's the thing about "strategies." Almost all of them are compromises. They are ways for you to pick out all the questions you can answer, and leave the hard ones. This will mean that you will struggle to score above 30 in this section.

If you need a score of more than 30, be prepared to practice very hard! Read this book thoroughly, and make sure you have practiced this section at least 15 times before test day. That sounds like a lot, but remember that you've already done at least two tests. If you want to write the test in three months' time, that's only a little more than one section per week.

The most important thing with your timing strategies is to practice them. Some of them can be complicated, and if you're struggling to remember your strategy, that takes up working memory (your ability to hold information in the front of your mind to work with it). This test is very taxing on working memory, so you don't want to waste time thinking about what your strategies are. Practice them so much that they become automatic!

That being said, let's look at some of the most common strategies. I've listed all the strategies I've ever heard of – from books, the Internet, my students, or ones I've come up with myself. I don't think all of them are good. In fact, in my experience, some can even hurt your score. I'm going to show you the pros and cons so you can decide for yourself, because some strategies are great for some people, but not for others.

1. Read the questions and not the passage. This can be a big timesaver, but you can also spend more time answering the questions because you don't know anything about what's going on. In my opinion, it's better to use HoVerCrafT, or some version of it to locate the relevant facts, then go to the questions. Even if you only manage H and V, the 30 seconds it will take you to do that are worth it. Experiment with this strategy and see what works for you. Perhaps finding H and V works. Perhaps you find it helpful to go straight to the questions when you're on the last passage and possibly running out of time.

2. Look only for questions that refer to a specific part of the passage. For example, "According to table 3 ...." If you do this for the whole passage, you will struggle to get more than half the questions right. If that's what you're aiming for, then go ahead. But if you need a higher score, this is a strategy that you should employ only if you're running out of time. This can also be a little deceptive, because although you're being pointed to a certain part of the passage, you might also need information from elsewhere in the passage.

3. HoVerCrafT! Of course I like this one! I spent the whole of my first chapter discussing it. The benefits are that it is based on the scientific method, so it's guaranteed to work every time. It would not be possible to create a passage in this test that didn't have a hypothesis, variables, trends or conclusions! The disadvantage is that it takes time to practice and implement this strategy. It can be a lot to think about initially. But it will help you every time.

4. Skip questions you don't understand. This could include very wordy questions, ones that ask you to look at several pieces of information together or just generally difficult questions. This is a pretty broad strategy, so it depends how you apply it. If you need above a 28/36, you can't reasonably skip more than about one question per passage (allowing for you to make some genuine mistakes as well). If you need 21-28 (you can skip 2-3 questions. Put a star by these questions and come back to them.

5. Choose one passage to skip, based on topic. For example, if you haven't studied physics, but have studied biology, you should find biological passages slightly easier to understand. When you see a physics passage, think about skipping it. Look ahead in the test to see what else is there, and see if that looks like the hardest passage. Spend a maximum of one minute doing this, because otherwise you could use that time to answer questions, and therefore get a better score. As soon as you decide to skip a passage, fill in the bubble sheet for that section so you don't forget later and get confused!

6. The 5-6-7 or the 7-6-5. Some people advocate doing the 5 question passages first, followed by the 6, then the 7. Or the other way around. To be honest, I'm not sure of the sense in the 5-6-7. The theory behind this strategy is that time spend reading the passage doesn't get you any marks - only time spent answering the questions. So you should do the passages that have the highest number of questions first. Make sure you practice this one, as if you don't do the passages in order, your bubble sheet could get messy! Some people also think the 5 question passages are easier. I haven't seen that trend personally.

7. The first three questions only. Sometimes the first three questions on a given passage are the easiest, and the next few are hard. If this is the case, then it makes sense to do only the first three easy questions. Personally, I'm not sure how much truth there is in this. It could easily be the other way around, and you put a lot of time investment into reading a passage if you're only going to attempt three questions. I think it would be better to pick the easier questions yourself, which basically turns this strategy into skipping questions you don't understand, which is usually a good idea!

8. Skip conflicting viewpoints passages. Some people hate these! They are different from the other passages, so if you always do worse on these than other passages, consider skipping them altogether. You might want to consider this strategy if your score on the Reading section is one of your lower ones, as it's most similar to the Reading section. The downside here is that these passages usually have seven questions, so you're already limiting yourself to scoring a maximum of 33/40. Yes, you could get some right by guessing, but statistically you can only expect to get 1-2 out of 7. As above, if you decide to skip a conflicting viewpoints passage, fill in the bubble sheet for it straight away.

9. Use a halfway marker. This is one of the best strategies, because it's not a compromise. The test takes 35 minutes, so when you begin, look at your start time, and add 17 minutes. Write this time at the top of passage four. If you have a six-passage test, the beginning of passage 4 is exactly the halfway point. If you have seven passages, your halfway point is about when you've read passage 4 and are just beginning the questions. Now you know whether you need to speed up or slow down by just checking the clock when you get to your halfway marker. This is much more useful than the five minutes' warning that you get at the end (also some proctors forget to give you that anyway!). There's not much you can do with five minutes, but there's a lot you can do with do with 17 minutes! This strategy is so useful that I recommend it for everybody. Even if you normally have no problem finishing the test, this is your insurance policy. This is a strategy that's not a compromise, and so it's one I really like!

Now that you've read over all of these, think carefully about which strategies you think would work for you. Choose two, and try them, either one at a time, or both together, on two practice tests. (Some of these strategies can be paired together, others can't.)

Take up your test. Think about whether you liked the strategy or not, and why. Track changes with this table. I've included space for your first two tests.

	Questions completed in 35 minutes	Amount of extra time needed	Raw score	Scaled score	Strategies used
Test 1			/40	/36	none
Test 2			/40	/36	none
			/40	/36	
			/40	/36	
			/40	/36	
			/40	/36	

If anything changed, or if you think the strategies are helpful, keep going. Perhaps try different strategies. You should have some idea about what is likely to work for you. This is the most important thing you need to do for the test! The Scientific Reasoning section takes perseverance! From now until you first intend to write the test, do one science practice section per week at minimum.

What if my score just isn't changing?

Sometimes, students work very hard to improve their score on the Scientific Reasoning sections, and it just doesn't change. If this is you, you have two options. One is to switch to the SAT, which doesn't have this section. Your other option is to get some outside help. Be aware that for this section, if you've followed all my advice to this point, there may not be much you can do. Expert tutoring helps a lot for Math and English, but less so for Reading and Scientific Reasoning. You might have some specific problem that a tutor can really help you with, but be wary of anyone promising a magical score improvement! I have written about how to choose a tutor or prep program, and whether to consider writing the SAT, in my Useful Things appendix.

What next?

At the beginning of this book, I stated three things that were necessary for you to get the score you want:

- The right approach

- The right timing strategies

- The right knowledge

We've covered the first two points, and for some people that may be enough. However, the ACT does include some questions that require specific knowledge, which can't be reasoned out from the test, and even some questions that are math based. If you feel that you need help in these areas, keep reading. I have outlined core topics in biology, chemistry, physics, earth and space science, and math, with ACT style practice passages to test what you've learned. Bear in mind that these really are outlines! For a lot of the topics I've given, it would be preferable to know more detail.

Lastly, make sure you check out the Useful Things appendix – it's called that for a reason!

The Knowledge

Now that you understand the test and are sure you have the right approach and strategy, it's time to brush up on your knowledge. I realize you may have already used this section as a reference, or that you may not need it at all, but here it is just in case! I have to emphasize here, again, that this is not a knowledge test. However, there are a couple of questions that do require basic, direct knowledge. Be aware that this section is not comprehensive – in some cases, it may help to know more about the topic than what I've outlined. I've pointed this out for you when I think you should know more than what I've written. Having familiarity with scientific process and ideas will really help you to understand the aim of the questions though. That's partly why I base my "approach" section around the scientific method – it's the process and discipline of thinking that you need to follow. It's also helpful not to be going into the test with misconceptions about scientific theories. That will not help your reasoning process!

Here's what's in this section:

- Chemistry
    - o Atoms, mass, moles and molecules
    - o Nuclear chemistry
    - o Acids and bases
    - o Titration
    - o Solubility
    - o Diffusion and osmosis

- Biology
    - o Cells and organelles
    - o Classifying living things
    - o Genetics
    - o Evolution, natural selection and adaptation

- Earth and space
    - o Climate

- o   Geology

- o   Astronomy

- Physics

    - o   Electricity

    - o   Energy and the laws of motion

    - o   Kinetic theory and gas laws

- Measurement

- Math

Chemistry

Atoms, mass, moles and molecules

An atom has a nucleus, which is composed of protons and neutrons. Around the nucleus are electrons. These are very far away from the nucleus, and are often depicted as moving in circular orbits, as in the diagram on the right. This isn't quite true, but it's a good enough model a lot of the time. According to this model, you can fit two electrons in the first shell, eight in the second and eight in the third. Again, this isn't actually true, but it's a good place to start.

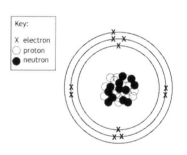

Particle	Mass	Charge	What's it made of?
Proton	1	+1	Smaller particles called quarks
Neutron	1	0	Also made of quarks
Electron	0	−1	Nothing – an electron is a fundamental particle. It's just an electon.

The periodic table is a list of all the different types of atoms in order of how many protons they have (atomic number). It also states their masses. This is a section of the periodic table that denotes sodium, which has the symbol Na (some of the element symbols are from Latin). Sodium has 11 protons, and 23 neutrons and protons together, and therefore 12 neutrons. Don't worry, you don't have to memorize anything that appears on the periodic table!

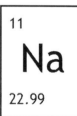

If you would like to know the mass of an atom or a molecule, you can just look it up in the periodic table. For a molecule, just add the masses of all the atoms in the molecule (e.g., to find the mass of copper sulfate, $CuSO_4$, just add the mass of copper, sulfate and 4 × the mass of oxygen). Since atoms are actually very small, the masses listed are for a very large number of atoms. For example, this very large number of atoms, if they were carbon atoms, would weigh about 12 g. If that same number of atoms were gold, they would weigh about 197 g. This very large number is called a mole, and its actual value is 6.022×10^{23} (it's known as Avogadro's number). Think of it like a dozen. We refer to a dozen eggs, meaning 12 eggs. If we refer to a mole of sodium, it means 6.022×10^{23} atoms.

You might have wondered why the mass number for sodium is not an integer (whole number). This is because not all sodium atoms have the same number of neutrons. On average, sodium atoms have 12 neutrons, but some will have less, and some will have more. What's recorded on the periodic table is an average mass of the different versions. These different versions of elements are called isotopes. Some isotopes are radioactive (see below).

Now, you don't need to know this much detail for the ACT, but what you do need to know is that 50 g of water (H_2O) would contain fewer atoms than 50 g of hydrogen (H_2), because hydrogen is much lighter than water.

Remember that atoms react to form molecules by losing or gaining electrons. Sometimes they are fully lost/gained to another atom. This is an ionic bond. Sometimes electrons are shared – this is a covalent, or molecular, bond. The position of the electrons in a bond between two atoms is determined by electronegativity. How equally the electrons are shared is determined by the different in electronegativity between the two atoms.

It's a good idea if you know this stuff very thoroughly! Recap from your textbook or notes if necessary.

Nuclear chemistry

Atoms that are either very large or have many neutrons, are unstable. This means that they are likely to decay radioactively. There are three types of decay – alpha, beta and gamma decay, and gamma decay usually accompanies the other two types. It's not possible to predict exactly when an atom will decay, but since atoms are so small, a large amount of them is actually quite predictable. The definition of half-life is the amount of time taken for the substance to decay to half its original amount.

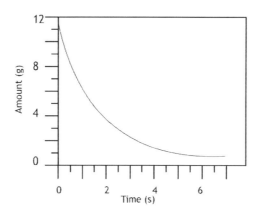

This graph demonstrates that behavior. Compare the amount of substance at 2 seconds with the amount at 4 seconds. There is about half as much after 2 seconds. This is because the half-life of this particular isotope is 2 seconds.

Self-test 1

1. Use a periodic table to calculate the approximate number of neutrons in sodium, iron, neon and silver.

2. Fill in this table without looking back at the previous page:

Particle	Mass	Charge
Proton		
Neutron		
Electron		

3. Which contains more calcium, 14 g of $CaCO_3$ or 14 g of $CaCl_2$?

4. If I have 10 g of Americium-241, and its half-life is 432 years, how much will I have after 1296 years?

5. If 4 g of element X takes 3 years to decay to 1 g, what is its half-life?

Answers on page 77.

Acids and bases

This is a fundamental concept for ACT scientific reasoning – it comes up time and time again!

Some substances are acidic, some are basic (alkaline) and some are neutral. We can measure the pH of a compound to find out which it is. If its pH is between 0-7, we classify it as acidic. If it's 7-14, it's alkali. If it's 7, it's neutral[1].

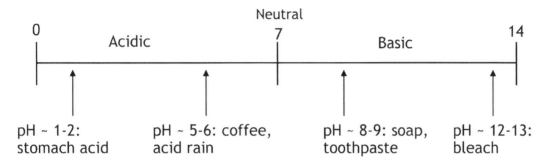

Acids are usually defined as substances that can give away an H+ ion to other substances. They react with metals and carbonates, taste sour, conduct electricity and turn litmus paper red. Litmus paper is one type of indicator. An indicator is a substance that changes color depending on the acidity/basicity of the solution it's in.

Bases, or alkalis, are usually defined as substances that can accept an H+ ion from acids. They also conduct electricity, but they taste bitter, and turn litmus paper blue.

Acids and bases react in a neutralization reaction: acid + base → ionic compound + water

For example: $HCl + NaOH \rightarrow NaCl + H_2O$

Common acids	Common bases
Sulfuric acid: H_2SO_4	Sodium hydroxide: NaOH
Hydrochloric acid: HCl	Potassium hydroxide: KOH
Phosphoric acid: H_3PO_4	Sodium hydrogencarbonate: $NaHCO_3$
Nitric acid: HNO_3	Ammonia: NH_3

An acid **always** has H somewhere in its formula. A base **often**, but not always, has OH (hydroxide) somewhere in its formula.

---

1   The pH formula is $pH = -\log_{10}[H^+]$, where $[H^+]$ is the concentration of hydrogen ions.

Titration

Titration (also called volumetric analysis) is a common laboratory method of quantitative chemical analysis (i.e. doing math with chemistry) that is used to determine the unknown concentration of a known reactant.

If you know that 20 g of A reacts with 40 g of B, and you have a solution that contains 80 g of B plus some unknown amount of A, then if half the A solution reacts with all of the B solution, you know that half the A solution contains 40 g of A. Therefore the whole solution contains 80 g of A.

Here's the experimental set-up that you might see. Sometimes they don't give you a diagram because the titration is done using specialized equipment. The substance with unknown concentration goes in the conical flask, and the substance of known concentration is put in the burette. The burette is marked with measurements. Both solutions must be measured very accurately.

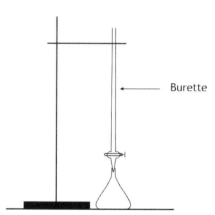

Burette

Here's the principle of titration. Start with a balanced chemical equation. Let's say X and Y react together in a 1:2 ratio:

$$X + 2Y \rightarrow Z + H_2O$$

If we have a known amount of X, we can find out how much Y we have if we react the two together, adding as much X as we can until the reaction is done. We just need something to tell us when the reaction is complete. For an acid base reaction, this is easy, because we can use an indicator (a substance that changes color depending on the pH). It's worth finding a titration video to see this in action! On the next page is an ACT style titration passage to test your skills.

4 ○ ○ ○ ○ ○ ○ ○ ○

Passage I

Biochemical oxygen demand (BOD) is a measure of dissolved oxygen that is needed for aquatic microbial organisms to break down organic matter present in water. It is used as an indicator of pollution, as the change in oxygen levels reflects the amount of organic matter (the pollutant) metabolized by microbes in the water.

BOD is defined as the amount of oxygen used from a liter of water at 20°C in five days. Table 1 shows BOD values for water at various levels of pollution.

BOD (mg/L)	Water condition
< 2	very clean
2–8	moderate pollution
> 8	severely polluted

Table 1

BOD is calculated by measuring the change in dissolved oxygen (DO) content over a five-day interval

Dissolved oxygen is measured by a titration method. The sample of river water is diluted with purified water, and prepared for titration by addition of sulfuric acid and alkali-iodide-azide reagent. It is then titrated with sodium thiosulfate, using starch as an indicator.

Experiment 1

Analysts conducted a series of studies at various points along a river to determine the current levels of pollution in the water. Figure 1 shows a map of the region.

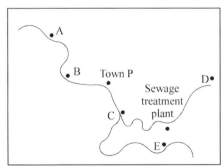

Figure 1

The analysts measured initial DO and final DO by titration, and used these results to calculate BOD. Their results are shown in Table 2.

	Initial DO (mg/L)	Final DO (mg/L)	BOD (mg/L)
A	3	2	1
B	3	2	1
C	10	4	4
D	12	3	7
E	11	4	5

Table 2

1. Which of the points A – E is likely furthest upstream (closest to river source)?

   A. A
   B. B
   C. C
   D. D

2. One of the analysts claims that there may be groundwater contamination at site E from the sewage treatment plant. Is she correct?

   A. Yes, because the BOD at E is higher than at C.
   B. Yes, because the BOD at E is lower than at C.
   C. No, because the BOD at E is higher than at D.
   D. Yes, because the BOD at E is lower than at D.

3. A student working with the analysts wishes to explain how BOD relates to DO. Which statement best describes the relationship?

   A. A high initial DO value gives a high BOD because BOD is higher when more oxygen is initially present.
   B. A low final DO gives a low BOD because BOD reflects how much oxygen is left after five days.
   C. BOD shows how much DO pollution is present in the water.
   D. The difference between initial and final DO gives the BOD because BOD is a reflection of how much oxygen is consumed.

Answers on page 77.

Solubility

A solute (e.g. sugar) dissolves in a solvent (e.g. water) to make a solution. Solubility depends on temperature (you can dissolve more sugar in hot water than in cold). This can be represented by a solubility curve, like the one on the right. You can also work out, from the scale on the y axis, how much of the substance will dissolve in 50 g of water by reading the graph and dividing the number by 2.

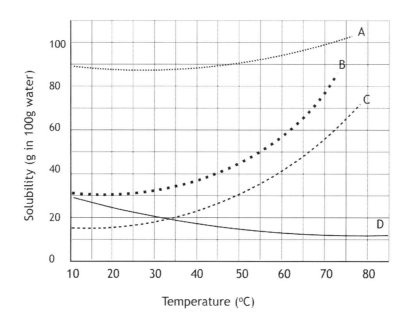

1. How much of substance A dissolves in 100 g water at 70°C?

2. How much of substance C dissolves in 50 g water at 25°C?

Answers on page 77.

Diffusion and osmosis

Diffusion is the process by which particles spread from an area of low concentration to an area of high concentration. It happens in liquids and gases, and in gases it's the reason why smells reach your nose! Osmosis is the process by which water moves to equalize concentration. Water will move from an area of low concentration to an area of high concentration. Yes, this is the opposite of diffusion, because a high concentration of water is normally referred to as a low concentration of solute. Read this paragraph again if you need to!

Substances can enter cells by diffusion (sometimes) and water can leave cells by osmosis. Comparing two solutions, the more concentrated one is said to be hypertonic. The less concentrated one is said to be hypotonic. If they have the same concentration, they are isotonic.

This is a really important concept! If your blood is hypotonic with respect to your cells, you are dehydrated, and water is likely to move out of your cells into your blood. This works the other way around too. This is why IV drips in hospitals are saline solution, not just pure water – they need to be isotonic with your blood.

Again, make sure you really understand this. It's quite foundational to many biological and chemical processes.

Biology

Cells and organelles

Biology is the study of living organisms. Organisms are made up of organs, which are connected in organ systems (e.g. the respiratory system). Organs are made up of tissues, and tissues are made up of cells.

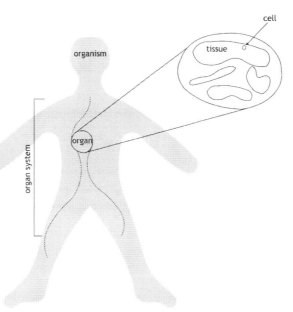

Organisms are also classified according to their cell types. Prokaryotes are made of cells that don't have a nucleus, whereas eukaryote cells do have a nucleus. Prokaryotes are comparatively simple organisms such as bacteria, whereas eukaryotes are higher order organisms such as plants, animals and humans.

There are several structures within cells (confusingly called organelles!) that you should know about.

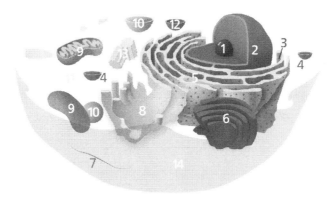

- The cell membrane (14) surrounds the cell and regulates what goes in and out of the cell.

- The nucleus (2) of the cell contains the genetic material for the cell. It is surrounded by a membrane in eukaryotes. Prokaryotes sometimes have what is referred to as a nuclear region. This is where its genetic material is found. The nucleolus (1) surrounds the nucleus.

- A vacuole (10) is a fluid-filled structure within a cell that helps maintain the shape of the cell. It's much larger in plants, because they don't have a skeleton.

- Mitochondria (9) are important organelles in the cell. They are part of a long chain of reactions that turn glucose into energy for the cell.

- Ribosomes (3) are also important – they synthesize proteins from instructions contained in DNA. Proteins carry out many different functions in the cell.

- The cytoplasm (11) is the fluid in the cell. It contains all sorts of dissolved particles and enzymes, which the cell uses.

- The cytoplasm contains vesicles (4), which transport things in the cell.

- The cytoskeleton (7) extends throughout the cell, and has many different functions, including structural support for the cell.

- The lysosome (12) breaks down large molecules

- The centrosome (13) helps to organize mitosis.

- The Golgi apparatus (6) packages and distributes proteins.

- There are two types of endoplasmic reticulum, rough (5) and smooth (8). The rough endoplasmic reticulum is studded with ribosomes, and both the rough and smooth ER are responsible for packing and folding proteins.

You need to know cells and organelles quite thoroughly, so make sure you know all of the information that's here!

Classifying living things

Biologists classify living things in order to determine their relationships. Every known organism has a two-part Latin name – for example, humans are *Homo sapiens*. *Sapiens* refers to the species, *homo* to the genus. Their classification is known as phylogeny. This diagram shows the phylogeny of some species in the family hyaenidae, which includes hyenas.

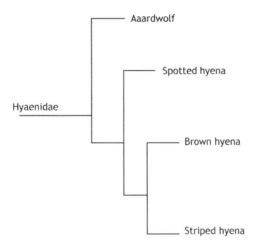

A slightly different type of diagram is a cladogram, which shows the evolutionary relationships between the species.

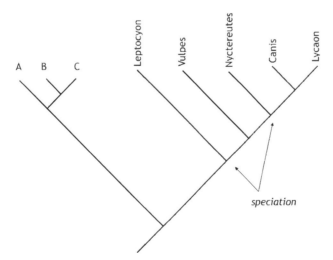

Part of the cladogram above shows the relationship between some different genera[2] - *Vulpes* (animals such as foxes), *Lycaon* (animals such as the African Hunting dog) and *Canis* (wolves, dogs, coyotes, etc.). Cladograms can be drawn for all levels of the taxonomic classification. This one shows different genera, but it could also show different species.

Each node of the cladogram indicates where a speciation (formation of a new species) happened. This also shows us which species are most closely related - species B and C on the diagram share a common ancestor which is not shared by species A, but species A, B and C do all have a common ancestor.

You may also be asked to use a dichotomous key to identify a species. A dichotomous key is a series of yes/no questions that identify the organism. For example, if you are looking at some bacteria under a microscope and trying to identify them, you might use the following questions:

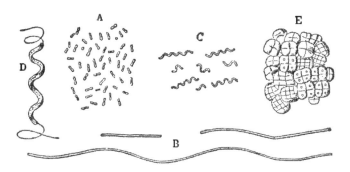

1. Is it spiral shaped? If yes, go to 2. If no, go to 3.

2. Is its diameter the same all the way along? If yes, it's C. If no, it's D.

3. Is it longer than it is wide? If no, it's E. If yes, go to 4.

4. Does it bulge at the ends? If yes, it's A. If no, it's B.

You should have now successfully classified it as one of the above.

---

2   The plural of genus is genera.

Genetics

This is a key topic to understand for ACT science! It would be helpful to know more than what is outlined here, so if you have studied genetics in more detail, take some time to review your notes on it. If you haven't, it may be a good idea to read up on it a little if you are aiming to get more than 35/40 on the ACT Scientific Reasoning.

Proteins are chemicals, made up of amino acids that do specific jobs in cells, for example hemoglobin is the protein in your blood that carries oxygen, and is also what gives blood its red color. Did you know that the blood of mollusks and some arthropods (e.g. crabs) is blue? Instead of hemoglobin, their blood contains hemocyanin. Proteins are made from a set of instructions contained in the nucleus of cells, called DNA.

DNA is made up of four different bases, shortened to A, T, C and G. They go in pairs, so A is always paired with T, and C is always paired with G. There are two strands in DNA, which fit together like a zipper, because of this pairing. Because of the pairing, the two strands are sort of copies of each other, which prevents mistakes in your genetic code. Each set of three base pairs is called a codon, and one codon is an instruction for one amino acid. When a protein needs to be made, special molecules read the DNA to figure out what amino acids to use. In this diagram, you can see the base pairs and the double helix spiral (bottom of the diagram). This is wound around molecular beads, called histones. Once wound, the "beads on a string" are referred to as nucleosomes. This is eventually wound into a shape called a chromosome. DNA is not in the chromosome formation most of the time; in fact, a lot of the time it is unwound.

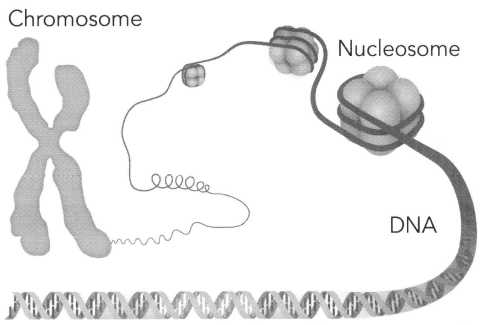

Image credit: Thomas Splettstoesser, www.scistyle.com

Humans have 22 pairs of chromosomes, plus either XX (females) or XY (males). Different regions of chromosomes are called genes. Usually, each gene codes for one or more proteins.

An allele is a version of a gene. For example, your eye color genes may be the blue allele, or the brown allele. Alleles can be dominant or recessive. For any given gene, you inherit one allele from your mother, and one from your father. This is called your genotype – the set of alleles that you have.

A karyotype is shown below. This is what you see when you look at someone's DNA using a test or sequencing method. Two karyotypes from the same person should be identical, and karyotypes from closely related people should be quite similar. This is the karyotype of a genetically normal human male.

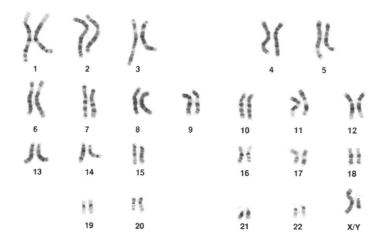

Image credit: National Cancer Institute, 1997

On the ACT Scientific Reasoning, you may see a Punnett square, which is a tool for working out the genetic traits of the offspring of two parents. Letters are used to denote the different alleles: capital letters for dominant alleles and lower case for recessive. In this one, both parents have a Gg genotype. We call this heterozygous, because the two alleles are different. If the two alleles are the same, we refer to this as homozygous.

Let's say this gene is for attached earlobes, with the dominant allele (G) meaning attached earlobes. Both parents have attached earlobes because they are both Gg (G dominates over g). Three-quarters of their children have attached earlobes too (GG, Gg and Gg), but one quarter has unattached – the child with gg genotype.

	G	g
G	GG	Gg
g	Gg	gg

4

Passage II

Cystic fibrosis is a genetic disorder caused by a mutation in the gene for CTFR protein which regulates the viscosity (thickness) of secretions such as sweat, mucus and digestive juices.

People who suffer from cystic fibrosis produce very thick mucus, which can damage the lungs, leading to lung infections, which reduce life expectancy.

Cystic fibrosis is an autosomal recessive disorder, which means that an individual must inherit two alleles of the defective gene – one from each parent.

Researchers conducted a series of studies to look at patterns of inheritance in cystic fibrosis. They have used the symbol C for the normal CTFR allele, and c for the defective CTFR gene.

Study 1

The Vermeer family has four children, one of whom has cystic fibrosis (child 4). Possible genotypes for their children are shown:

Child 1: CC or Cc
Child 2: CC or Cc
Child 3: CC or Cc
Child 4: cc

Study 2

The Vermeer family would like to know whether it is likely that their grandchildren will have cystic fibrosis. It is assumed that they will have children with a carrier of cystic fibrosis (genotype Cc).

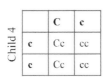
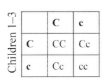
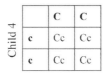

Study 3

The researchers conducted a population study using the Hardy-Weinberg equation, which models allele frequency in a population. They found the following:

Cystic fibrosis sufferers: 0.03%
Carriers of cycstic fibrosis: 3.6%
Unaffected: 96.3%

1. What is the most likely genotype of the Vermeer parents in Study 1?

   A. CC and CC
   B. cc and cc
   C. Cc and CC
   D. Cc and cc

2. Child 1 has a genetic test and finds that he has genotype Cc. If he has children with someone of genotype Cc, what percentage of their children will be expected to be carriers of cystic fibrosis and have cycstic fibrosis?

   A. Carriers: 50%   Cystic fibrosis: 25%
   B. Carriers: 25%   Cystic fibrosis: 50%
   C. Carriers: 75%   Cystic fibrosis: 25%
   D. Carriers: 100% Cystic fibrosis: 0%

3. Based on Study 3, is it possible that two people who do not have cystic fibrosis could have a child with cystic fibrosis?

   A. Yes, because 3.6% of people are carriers of an allele for cystic fibrosis.
   B. Yes, because 0.03% of people have cystic fibrosis.
   C. No, because only 0.03% of people have cystic fibrosis.
   D. No, because only 3.6% of people are carriers of an allele for cystic fibrosis.

Answers on page 77.

Evolution, natural selection and adaptation

Natural selection is the theory that some adaptations are beneficial for living in a certain environment, and that organisms with those adaptations are most likely to survive, reproduce, and therefore pass on these beneficial adaptations. Over time, the species will show a greater prevalence of that adaptation.

Let's take, for example, a herd of cows that live in a marshy region. One year, there is much more rain than usual. Some of the cows have wider feet than others, and hence are able to move and graze faster, without getting stuck in the marsh. These cows are more likely to survive, because they are beneficially adapted for their environment. If the marshy, wet conditions continue, after a period of time, the cow herd will likely be made up of more cows with wide, flat feet.

A common misinterpretation of this is to say something like: "Marshy conditions make the cows grow wider feet." This isn't what happens! Whether the cows have wide feet or not is initially random. But over time, a change in the environment confers an advantage on the wide-footed cows, and so that advantage is selected for.

The theory of evolution states that the formation and development of new species happens over a long period of time by the process of natural selection. Again, for the ACT, this is a principle that you should understand thoroughly.

Self-test 2

1. What is the function of a ribosome?

2. Describe the shape of the DNA molecule.

3. What is speciation?

4. Which organelles do plant cells have that animal cells do not have?

5. True or False:

    a. Humans have a total of 44 chromosomes

    b. The mitochondria is responsible for protein transport

    c. DNA is made of four base pairs

    d. Alleles come in two types: dominant and reduced

    e. Proteins are made of amino acids

  f. Prokaryotic cells have a nucleus

  g. Photosynthesis takes place in the cytoplasm

  h. Natural selection explains how organisms that have beneficial characteristics for their particular environment are more likely to survive and pass on these characteristics, leading to a species that is overall better adapted for its environment.

Answers on page 77.

Earth and space

Climate

Climate is different from weather. Weather is what comes after the news – it's what's happening right now! Climate is the general pattern of weather over a number of years. Climatologists might measure long-term patterns in temperature, humidity, precipitation, atmospheric pressure, or wind speed and direction.

The climate of a location is affected by its latitude (how far north or south it is), terrain, and altitude, as well as nearby water bodies and their currents. Climates can be classified according to the average and the typical ranges of different variables, most commonly temperature and precipitation.

There are five components to a climate system – atmosphere (air), hydrosphere (water – lakes, rivers, ocean, etc.), lithosphere (surface of the earth), biosphere (living parts of the climate) and, if applicable, cryosphere (snow, ice or other frozen water). Different locations have different climates based on their balance of these five components. You don't need to know any of this specific terminology for the ACT Scientific Reasoning, but it will be helpful to have an overview. Climate is quite a broad topic, so it may be worth knowing a little more than this. If these three paragraphs about climate were completely new information to you, then try to read a bit more about climate. Resources for the AP Environmental Science course may be helpful here, but this is only a necessary step if you are looking for a very high score.

Geology

There are often some geology-based passages on the ACT Scientific Reasoning. It's helpful to know a little bit about this, but your knowledge can be quite minimal. The Earth is (almost) a sphere, and it comes in layers, like this:

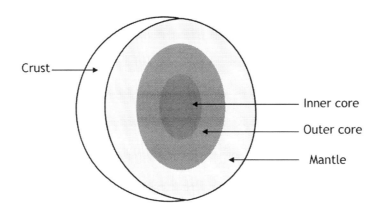

The crust is between about 0-60 km thick, depending on where you are in the world. Below that is the mantle, which is made of a sort of thick fluid, known as magma. The outer core is liquid iron and nickel, which is the reason why the Earth has a magnetic field. Because these metals are in liquid form, the magnetic field of the Earth moves a bit over time. The inner core is solid iron and nickel.

The crust of the Earth is made of a number of tectonic plates. You can see these on this overlaid map:

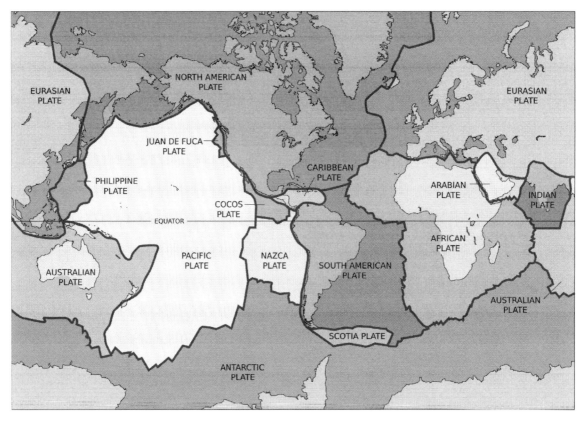

Image produced by the US Geological Survey

Because these plates are sitting on the mantle, which moves, they move too. This usually happens gradually, but when it happens suddenly, there is an earthquake. Some of these plates are moving away from each other, creating gaps in the crust of the Earth. Some are moving towards each other, which creates mountain ranges such as the Himalayas.

In places where the crust of the Earth is thin, volcanoes are common. Volcanoes happen when magma is compressed, and rises to the surface of the Earth suddenly. When the Earth's crust is thin, water that is piped down through the crust can heat up quite quickly. This can cause natural hot springs, and can also be used to create geothermal energy.

The crust of the Earth is made of rocks and soil. Soil and other loose small particles lie on the surface. Below that is bedrock – a layer of solid rock. The foundations of skyscrapers usually have to be anchored in the bedrock, but depending on the local geology, this may be quite far below the surface.

There are three kinds of rock – igneous, sedimentary and metamorphic. They are related by the rock cycle:

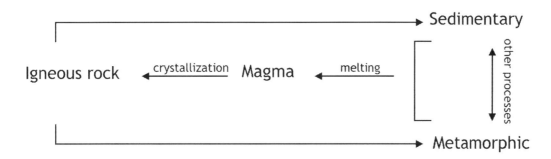

The crystallization process turns magma (molten rock) into igneous rock. Other geological processes can turn igneous rock into either sedimentary or metamorphic rock. When either of these melt, magma is formed.

There are many kinds of soil, including sand, clay, silt, peat, etc. Soil contains decayed organic matter: the remains of dead animals, insects and plants that are broken down by bacteria that live in the soil. It also contains very small pieces of rock – essentially sand. The balance of these components, and the composition of the rocks, gives the overall composition of the soil. If you walk in rural areas, you'll probably have seen some different soil types. You don't need to know the specific kinds, but it's a good idea to at least know that there are different types of soil!

Astronomy

Astronomy is the study of stars, planets and other objects in space. A star is a dense ball of gas, which is so large that the force of its own gravity holds it together under pressure so great that nuclear reactions happen in the center. The energy that is given off by these reactions is the light we see from the star. A planet is an object that orbits a star. In our solar system (i.e. the planets orbiting the Sun), some planets are rocky (like Earth), and others are gaseous (like Jupiter). Objects that orbit planets are known generally as satellites, but if they are natural and not man-made, they are usually referred to as moons. In this diagram, you can see a comet on the left. A comet is made of ice, burning dust and small rock, and they are sometimes visible in the night sky.

Image created by NASA

Orbits are usually elliptical (oval). They have what is called a "period" – the amount of time taken for the object to go around the planet/star once and return to its original position. They also have a radius[3].

Self-test 3

1. What is igneous rock?

2. What is a star made of?

---

3 Technically since they are not circular, they don't have a single radius. Instead, they are usually described by their semi-major axis: the largest of the possible radii of the object.

3. How many parts are there to the Earth? Give the name of each section.

4. What does latitude measure?

5. What is a satellite?

Answers on page 77.

Physics

Electricity

Electricity is a property of electrons, and one of the fundamental forces in the universe. A flow of electrons (or in fact any charged particle) is an electric current. Electrons are negatively charged particles, so when something loses electrons it becomes positively charged. An electric current only happens in a complete circuit, but small amounts of charge can be built up when two surfaces rub together and transfer some electrons (static electricity). Here are some definitions you should know:

- Charge is the difference in number of electrons. If a material gains two electrons, its charge will be –2. If a material loses two electrons, its charge will be +2.

- Conductors are low resistance materials that allow the flow of electrons easily, for example, metals such as copper.

- Insulators are high resistance materials that don't usually allow the flow of electricity, for example, rubber and plastics.

- If something is grounded, it means it is attached to a large object through which any excess charge dissipates.

- Electric current is how much charge is flowing past a point in a given time, that is, the rate of charged particles moving.

- Voltage is most easily thought of as the energy that the current has (but it's a little more complicated than this).

- Resistance is a measure of how freely charge can pass through an object. Insulators have high, or virtually infinite resistance.

Remember the basic principle of electric charges: opposite charges attract, like charges repel. If two objects both have a negative charge, they will move away from each other if they can.

There are two ways of connecting an electric circuit – in series, as on the right, or in parallel, as on the left. Current, voltage and resistance work differently in each case. If these diagrams look unfamiliar to you, search "circuit symbols" or "circuit diagrams."

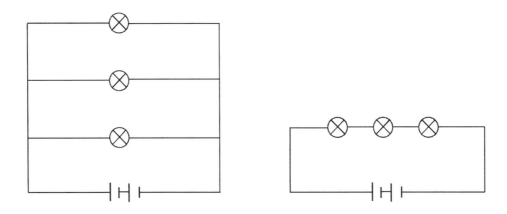

Energy and the laws of motion

The first law of thermodynamics states, in simple terms, that energy can't be created or destroyed; it can only be changed from one form into another. In order for this concept to make sense, sometimes we have to consider types of potential energy as well. For example, think about compressing a spring – you use energy to compress it, so the spring must contain that stored energy, which we call elastic potential energy. If you pick up a pencil, you give it gravitational potential energy, and when you drop it, that energy is transformed into kinetic energy plus a little bit of sound and heat energy when it hits the floor. Here are the types of energy:

- Light energy (which is really a form of electromagnetic energy)

- Kinetic energy (the energy of a moving object)

- Sound energy

- Heat energy (which is really kinetic energy of the atoms and molecules vibrating)

- Electrical potential energy (two charged objects have potential energy, which is proportional to the distance between them)

- Chemical potential energy (energy stored within chemical bonds)

- Elastic potential energy

- Gravitational potential energy

One concept often tested on the ACT is the conversion of kinetic energy to gravitational potential energy. Here's a diagram of a cart on a rollercoaster. What do you notice about the total energy at each point?

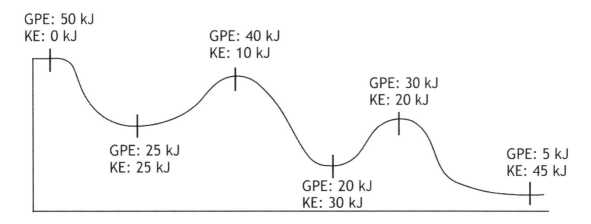

I hope you figured out that the total energy is the same at each point. In situations like this, as the cart loses gravitational potential energy (GPE), this is converted into kinetic energy (KE). In reality, there will be some loss of energy due to friction.

It's very important to know that **energy is not the same thing as force!**

Force is measured in Newtons (N), and it is a vector quantity, which means that it has to have a direction as well (think about it – if you're applying a force, it has to be in a certain direction!). Energy is measured in Joules (or in Newton metres if you like!), and doesn't have a direction. Energy is a number only quantity (also known as a scalar).

One other very important concept is momentum. An object's momentum is the product of its mass and its velocity. It has the symbol p, so $p = mv$. Larger, faster objects have more momentum than lighter, slower ones.

Laws of motion

Moving objects always follow certain rules, which were neatly summarized by Sir Isaac Newton.

1. If there are balanced forces acting on an object, it will move at a constant speed (which could include zero speed).

2. If unbalanced forces are applied to an object, it will accelerate (frictional force causes most objects to deaccelerate).

3. Also, every action has an equal and opposite reaction. If you stand on the desk, your weight

is pushing the desk downwards, and the desk is producing an opposing force to balance out your weight (unless of course it can't, in which case it will break!).

Physicists often represent forces in a free body diagram, as below. The top diagram is a free body diagram representing an object on a hill. The angle of the hill is 23°, and there are two forces acting on the object. There must be a rope attached to it, providing the upwards tension force. The weight of the object (which always acts directly downwards) is the second force.

In the diagram at the bottom, a sign is suspended by two ropes. There are three forces acting on this sign.

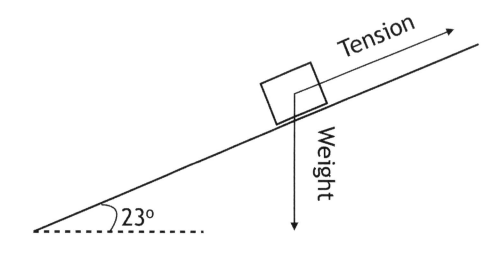

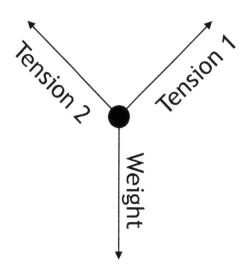

4

Passage III

A group of students decided to conduct a series of experiments to determine what factors affect the velocity of a cart as it rolls down a track. The students measured velocity using detectors situated at the points A – F below. Point A is at a height of 1 m above the floor, and the final velocity of the carts was recorded at point F, which is 0.15 m above the floor. The heights of points B, C, D and E are shown in the diagram.

The measured velocity values were used to calculate kinetic energy values, and the heights of the points were used to calculate gravitational potential energy values. Their set-up is shown in Figure 1.

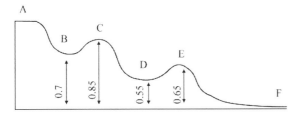

Figure 1

Experiment 1

The students constructed four carts of different masses (but same shape) and recorded their velocities as they rolled down the track. The results are shown in Table 1.

	Measured velocity				
	Point B	Point C	Point D	Point E	Point F
Cart 1 (10g)	5.88	2.94	8.82	6.86	16.6
Cart 2 (20g)	5.88	2.93	8.84	6.85	16.6
Cart 3 (30g)	5.87	2.93	8.8	6.83	16.6
Cart 4 (40g)	5.86	2.87	8.79	6.83	16.6

Table 1

Experiment 2

The students repeated the procedure in Experiment 1, but they used a high friction surface for the track.

	Measured velocity				
	Point B	Point C	Point D	Point E	Point F
Cart 1 (10g)	5.66	2.87	8.80	6.83	16.4
Cart 2 (20g)	5.60	2.86	8.76	6.80	16.2
Cart 3 (30g)	5.55	2.84	8.72	6.58	16.1
Cart 4 (40g)	5.52	2.80	8.70	6.56	16.0

Table 2

Experiment 3

The students used the same procedure as in Experiment 1, but they raised the height of point A to 1.5 m.

	Measured velocity				
	Point B	Point C	Point D	Point E	Point F
Cart 1 (10g)	15.68	12.74	18.62	16.66	26.46
Cart 2 (20g)	15.67	12.72	18.62	16.65	26.44
Cart 3 (30g)	15.64	12.71	18.61	16.64	26.42
Cart 4 (40g)	15.63	12.70	18.58	16.62	26.40

Table 3

Questions:

1. What effect does the high friction surface have on the carts?
2. What effect does the mass have on the velocity of the cart? Is the effect large or small? Why does mass have this effect?
3. What happens when the intial height is raised? Why does this happen?

Answers on page 77.

Kinetic theory

Kinetic theory is a set of rules describing how molecules in fluids (liquids and gases) behave. It can explain many everyday observations, such as why balloons deflate, why you can smell a candle throughout the house, and why water boils faster at higher altitudes.

First, it's worth remembering that there are more than three states of matter. Another common one (besides solids, liquids and gases) is plasma, which is ionized gas. Plasmas conduct electricity. A plasma that you've certainly seen is fire. (Did you know that flames conduct electricity?[4]")

You might have seen solids, liquids and gases represented like this. This shows that gases are the least dense, and both liquids and gases fill the shapes of the containers that they are in. Both liquids and gases can be correctly known as fluids.

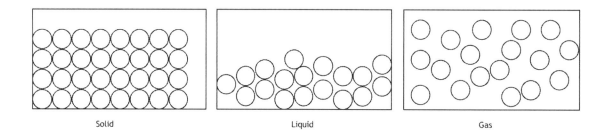

Solid   Liquid   Gas

According to kinetic theory, gases are made up of tiny particles that travel in straight lines until they hit something. When they hit each other, they may react. When they hit the walls of the container, they create pressure. The energy of a gas is usually thermal energy that is translated into kinetic energy of the molecules. Because kinetic energy depends on mass, larger particles in the gas travel more slowly. Chemical reactions may happen if the molecules collide with enough energy to react.

There are three main laws that talk about the behavior of gases. If you think enough about them, they are easy to visualize. Each has a mathematical formula, which I haven't given here; if you're interested, you can easily look up more information about gas laws.

- Boyle's law: pressure in a gas is inversely proportional to volume, at constant temperature. (Take a container of gas, and make the container smaller – that will increase the pressure.)

- Gay-Lussac's law (aka Pressure law): pressure is proportional to temperature, at constant

---

4   Science is cool! (Most of my footnotes are useful...don't give up on them.)

volume. (Take a container of gas and increase the temperature – the molecules will move faster, causing more collisions, creating more pressure.)

- Charles' law: volume is proportional to temperature, at constant pressure. (Take a container of gas, heat it, and the volume will increase.)

Now, if you were really thinking closely about these ideas, you might have spotted that it's hard to compress a gas and change the pressure but not the temperature. In fact, that doesn't really happen! This is where the ideal gas law comes in. The ideal gas law has the equation $pV = NRT$, where N is the number of moles of the gas and R is the molar gas constant (it has a value of 8.31). This shows you that all three variables (pressure, temperature and volume) are related. The problem with the ideal gas law is that no gases are truly ideal. Some, such as the noble gases of helium, neon, argon, krypton, xenon and radon, are pretty close.

You don't need to know any of this specifically, but it is a very good idea to have a brief overview of how gases behave. Try saying a quick summary of what you've just read to make sure it's sunk in. Here's a brief ACT style passage, but I've given you some non-multiple choice questions as well.

4

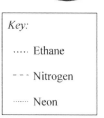

Key:

····· Ethane

- - - Nitrogen

········ Neon

Passage IV

A group of students wanted to investigate Gay-Lussac's law and the ideal gas law.

Experiment 1

The students first tested their gases to see whether they obeyed Gay-Lussac's law, which states that pressure is proportional to temperature in a closed system at constant volume. They filled a 0.5 L insulated container with each gas, sealed the container and heated each one. They used the equipment set-up shown in Figure 1.

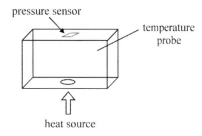

Figure 1

Their results are recorded in Table 1.

Temperature (K)	Pressure (kPa)		
	Neon	Nitrogen	Ethane
298	101	101	101
318	108	108	108
338	115	115	115
358	121	121	121

Table 1

Experiment 2

The students then used the same apparatus and the same gases to test which gas had the closest behavior to an ideal gas. They recorded the pressure and temperature changes continuously and plotted their results in Figure 2. The students used 1 mole of each gas. For an ideal gas, $pV = NRT$.

Answers on page 77.

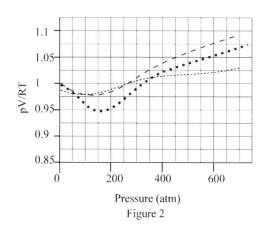

Figure 2

1. Which of the gases tested behaves most like an ideal gas?

    A. Ethane
    B. Nitrogen
    C. Neon
    D. All three behave ideally

2. Why did the students choose to test Gay-Lussac's law only?

3. Suggest a reason from your own knowledge for the gases not behaving ideally.

Measurement

Remember the third stage from the scientific method?

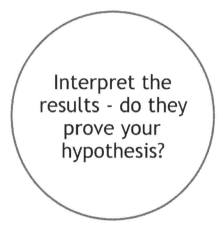

Whichever experiment you've done, the result comes in one of two forms – qualitative (word based, descriptive) or quantitative (numerical). Whenever you have quantitative results, you'll have measured them somehow, and measurements require units!

NB Be very careful with upper and lower case in units, for example T is temperature, but t is time! M is a prefix, meaning mega (see below), but m is the symbol for meters.

There is a standard unit of measurement for every quantity in science, known as the SI unit (for Système international). You don't need to know the ins and outs of this for the ACT, but it can save you a lot of time! There are also a lot of other units that could be used. For example, you might not know that mmHg is a unit of pressure.

Why are SI units so useful?

- If you put SI units into equations, you get SI units out!

- There are seven fundamental units that can express all other quantities (six are shown below).

- SI units can be modified to express very small or large quantities.

Every single thing you can measure has one of the units below, or a combination of them.

(NB I haven't included intensity of light, measured in candelas. You really don't need to know this one!)

Quantity	SI Unit	Non-SI Units
length	meters (m)	mile, feet, yards
pressure	kiloPascals (kPa)	atmospheres, psi, Torr, mmHg
mass	kilograms (kg)	pounds, stone, ounces
time	seconds (s)	minutes, hours
temperature	kelvin (K)	Fahrenheit, Celsius
electrical current	ampere/amps (A)	

You might notice that force isn't in the table. Force is usually measured in N (newtons), but it can also be measured in gm/s^2. This is just one example of a unit that is actually a combination of the fundamental units given above.

What if we want to talk about a really small or large quantity? We modify SI units according to standard rules. The modifications go in increasing order of size (small at the top).

Name	Symbol	Size
femto	f	10^{-15}
pico	p	10^{-12}
nano	n	10^{-9}
micro	μ	10^{-6}
milli	m	10^{-3}
kilo	k	10^3
mega	M	10^6
giga	G	10^9
tera	T	10^{12}

You know some of these already, for example 1000 meters is 1 km. 1000 km would be the same as 1 Mm – a megameter. Again, you don't need to memorize this, but you need to know that when you see μs, it's a very small fraction of a second. The most common SI modifications on the ACT are the small ones – nano, micro and milli.

Sometimes we modify SI units by size, using one of the non-standard prefixes, for example centimeters – because centimeters are a useful size.

Another really useful symbol to know is this one: Δ. It's a Greek capital delta, and it means "change in." For example, Δt means change in time. If you see ΔT in a table, you know that column represents the temperature change.

Math

You don't have to do that much math on the ACT Scientific Reasoning section. The hardest calculations are generally dividing by 10 or 2, and even those don't come up that often.

Just as a quick reminder, you also need to know that working out a percentage means taking a fraction and dividing by 100. For example, let's say you have a scale on a graph.

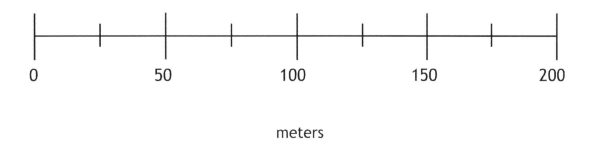

meters

Example 1. What percentage of the maximum value is 45 m?

   a. 50%

   b. 45%

   c. 65%

   d. 22.5%

This question requires you to calculate without a calculator. Take the shortcut and realize that if you divide by 200 then multiply by 100, you are really just dividing by 2, so that answer is d. You could see that like this:

$$\frac{45}{2 \times \cancel{100}} \times \cancel{100}$$

One slightly rarer type of question asks you to derive an expression based on the data given to you. Question 12 on the April 2016 paper, if you have access to it, is a great example of this. Don't worry if you don't have that test paper, the example I made below is just like it. This type of question tests something that will be quite straightforward to any physics student, but perhaps not so much otherwise. Try this:

Example 2. To stretch the spring by 4 m, a weight of 2 N was needed. If Sabrina wants to calculate the force constant of the spring, measured in N/m, which expression should she use?

a. 4 m × 2 N

b. 2 N ÷ 4 m

c. (2 N)² ÷ 4 m

d. 2 N ÷ 4 m

The correct answer is d. Your clue is in the question – notice how it gives you units of N/m? This tells you that to calculate this quantity, you must take a number in newtons and divide it by a number in meters. Physics is nice like that! This is sometimes called dimensional analysis. This is linked to the idea of SI units, and in fact all equations in SI units work like this. Think of distance, speed and time. If you want a distance (measured in meters), you must take a speed (meters per second) and multiply it by a time (seconds).

Do the math with the units and you'll see what I mean – the seconds cancel out:

$$m = \frac{m}{s} \times s$$

Here's the last type of math question you could see. I call it: "How an equation fits together." This is quite a mathematical concept, but there are a few questions on the ACT which ask you to pick the right equation from a table of data. You don't actually have to do any calculations here, but you need to understand the relationships between the variables. This is where your T (for trend, as in HoVerCrafT – look back to page 6 if you need to) comes in handy. Here's the key:

- If two variables both increase together, you should see them both in the numerator or both in the denominator of a given equation.

- If one increases while the other decreases, one will be in the numerator while the other is in the denominator.

Think carefully about why this is! This is not the kind of fact you should memorize, it's the kind of thing you should understand. The ACT tests this sort of concept in ways that you may not recognize, so it's essential to understand! Read over it a few times, come back to it if necessary, and if really necessary, ask someone to explain it to you more fully.

4

Passage V

Three students decided to measure all the factors that they thought might affect the speed of a clock pendulum. They made a model of a clock using a circular metal weight on a string as the pendulum bob. In their experiment, they varied the mass of the bob, the radius of the arc and the release height (measured vertically).

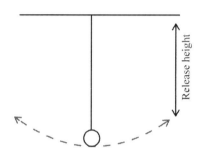

Figure 1

The students calculated predicted centripetal force and GPE (gravitational potential energy) at the center point of the pendulum's arc.

Their results are shown in Table 1.

1. Which of the following is the correct equation to relate radius of arc to centripetal force? (k is a constant of proportionality).

   A. $r_{arc} = k \times$ centripetal force
   B. $r_{arc} = k \div$ centripetal force
   C. $r_{arc} = k \times$ (centripetal force)^2
   D. $r_{arc} = k \div$ (centripetal force)^2

2. Which is the correct equation to relate release height to GPE at bottom of swing?

   A. $RH = k \times (GPE)^2$
   B. $RH = k \div GPE$
   C. $RH = k \times (GPE)^2 + 2$
   D. $RH = k \times GPE$

3. Which is the correct equation to relate mass of pendulum, centripetal force and GPE?

   A. $m_{pen} = k \times$ (centripetal force $\div$ GPE)
   B. $m_{pen} = k \times$ centripetal force $\times$ GPE
   C. $m_{pen} = k \div$ (centripetal force $\times$ GPE)
   D. $m_{pen} = (k \times GPE) \div$ centripetal force

Mass of pendulum	10	10	10	10	10	10	10	10	10	20	30	40	50
Radius of arc (m)	0.05	0.1	0.2	0.3	0.4	0.4	0.4	0.4	0.4	0.4	0.4	0.4	0.4
Release height (m)	0.05	0.05	0.05	0.05	0.05	0.05	0.1	0.15	0.2	0.25	0.25	0.25	0.25
Centripetal force (N)	0.196	0.098	0.049	0.033	0.025	0.049	0.074	0.098	0.123	0.245	0.368	0.490	0.613
GPE at arc centre (J)	0.5	0.5	0.5	0.5	0.5	0.5	1	1.5	2	5	7.5	10	12.5

Table 1

Answers on page 77.

Well done for getting this far. I sincerely hope that this book has got you where you need to be, and that I've helped you to understand and navigate this sometimes problematic section. Remember that the ACT is just a test – it's one more hoop that you have to jump through to reach your goals, whatever they are. If you've followed this book from start to finish, you've likely learned a little more than just ACT stuff though. I hope you've learned a little more about science, and a little more about learning too. That might be a big ambition for a test prep book to have, but it's partly why I wrote it. Take a minute to reflect on what you've gained.

Good luck!

The rest of this book is answers for the questions in this book, answer explanations for the five free online ACT papers, a list of question types, contents index and the Useful Things appendix.

Answers to Questions in This Book

Self-test 1

1. Subtract atomic number from mass number. Sodium has 12, iron has 30, neon has 10 and silver has 118.

2. Check your answer against the version of the table that's given on page 44.

3. There is more calcium in 14 g of $CaCl_2$, because the two chlorine atoms weigh less than three oxygens and a carbon, so proportionally, there's more calcium.

4. 1296 is 3 half-lives, so divide 10 g by 2 three times. You'll have 1.25 g left.

5. 4 g decaying to 1 g is halving twice, so its half-life must be 1.5 years.

Passage I: Titration

1. A. It's furthest upstream because it has the lowest pollution level (lowest BOD).

2. A. She is correct. There is nothing on the map between C and E that might raise pollution levels, and yet the BOD at E is higher than at C.

3. D. This is the most accurate explanation of BOD and DO, because BOD is the amount of oxygen used. DO is just the amount of oxygen, so you need to be looking at the difference in DO values.

Solubility

1. About 100 g

2. About 9 g (remember to halve the value you read from the graph as the question says 50 g water!).

Passage II: Genetics

1. D. Each parent must have at least one c allele for child 4 to be cc, which rules out A and C. If the parents' genotypes were cc and cc, all their children (as well as they themselves) would have cystic fibrosis.

2. A. Draw a Punnet square to answer this one. Cc are carriers, and cc have cystic fibrosis.

3. A. Yes, it is possible. If they are both the Cc genotype, then they have a 25% chance of having a child with cystic fibrosis; however, it is still quite unlikely.

Self-test 2

1. A ribosome is responsible for reading mRNA instructions and drawing amino acids together to create a protein.

2. The DNA molecule is a double helix.

3. Speciation is the development of a new species by an evolutionary process.

4. Plant cells have chloroplasts and cell walls, which are absent in animal cells. They often also have larger vacuoles.

5. F, F, T, F, T, F, F, T.

Self-test 3

1. Igneous rock is rock that's formed directly by a volcanic process.

2. A star is a dense cloud of dust and gas. Nuclear fusion is happening at its center.

3. Refer to the original diagram given.

4. Latitude is a measurement of how far north or south a location is. The equator has 0 latitude.

5. A satellite is any object that orbits a planet. Natural satellites are usually referred to as moons.

Passage III: Carts

1. The high friction surface reduces KE, and therefore v (as you would expect), but it has the greatest effect on the heaviest cart.

2. The mass doesn't seem to have an effect on the velocity of the cart, according to the data. This is true, because mass is in both the GPE and the KE equations, it effectively cancels out.

3. When the initial height is raised, all the velocities are greater. This is because the carts have more KE initially.

Passage IV: Gas laws

1. C. Neon. You should be looking for a straight line for the slope, as the passage tells you, and this is closest to it.

2. Boyle's law applies at constant temperature, and Charles' law applies at constant pressure, both of which are much harder to achieve experimentally than constant volume. (Don't worry if you didn't get this, it's hard!)

3. Gases don't behave ideally because of intermolecular forces between the molecules, among other things. Again, this is a hard question. If you want to know more about this, look it up.

Passage V: Pendulum

1. B. As radius increases, centripetal force decreases, but it's not a squared relationship. You should be looking at the first five columns of data to answer this.

2. D. Look at columns 7, 8 and 9 to answer this one. Both quantities increase together, and it's easy to see that it's not a squared relationship; they are being multiplied by 10.

3. B. Look at the last four columns here (where release height and radius or arc are constant). All the numbers increase together, so pick the equation that doesn't have division in it.

Answer Explanations

Find all these papers at prepACTSAT.com/ACT-official-tests

Practice test 1/Form 59F answer explanations

Passage I

My 30-second look at the passage gets me the following information:

- H: It's about metamorphic rock, which comes in different categories, aka facies.

- V: The graph has two y axes – pressure and depth (which are actually related if you think about it). The x axis is temperature.

- Table 1 relates facies type to metamorphic grade.

- Figure 2 classifies different kinds of rock by metamorphic grade.

- That means that Table 1 is your go-between anytime you want to find the likely facies of a type of rock.

1. C. Look at Figure 2. There are two rocks that are found only in medium grade and nowhere else – kyanite and staurolite, which is not an option.

2. J. Locate facies G in Figure 1, and check you're reading off the left y axis. This is the only value that's in the region of facies G.

3. C. Compare the labels on the two y axis carefully – the numbers only decrease going down, and they stay in the same order.

4. J. Look at Figure 2. The mineral plagioclase is present in rocks of all grade, hence it would not help you determine the grade of a rock at all.

5. A. If hornfels is formed at the earth's surface, it must be present only at very shallow depths. This means it would have to be facies A or B, and B is not an option.

Passage II

It's the conflicting viewpoints one – yay! My 30-second look at the passage gets me the following information:

- H: The scientists are discussing whether a certain object was a comet or an asteroid.

- C1: Scientist 1 thinks it was a comet because it left no crater, which is in turn because comets are made of dust and gas.

- C2: Scientist 2 thinks it was an asteroid, which flattened because of pressure (doesn't matter how!) and then exploded into tiny fragments, leaving no crater.

6. J. In your initial read, you spotted that they were disagreeing about comet vs. asteroid.

7. B. In the middle of Scientist 2's explanation, he or she states that, "a comet … would explode at an altitude much higher than 8 km."

8. G. Your clue is the word "vaporized" in Scientist 1's explanation. Vapor is another word for gas.

9. D. At the end of Scientist 2's explanation, he or she says that, "recovery is difficult due to the area's boggy soil."

10. H. In the sixth line of Scientist 2's explanation it says that the asteroid decelerated rapidly due to large a increase in its surface area. If it had not been flattened, this wouldn't have happened.

11. A. This one is best solved by eliminating the wrong choices. It can't be B, because that wouldn't explain the destruction of the forest. It can't be D because the object itself didn't strike the Earth's surface. C doesn't really make sense – it says in the introduction that the object exploded 8 km above the Earth's surface, so why would energy not be released until after? It has to be A.

12. G. H and J are not relevant to the comet striking the Earth! Scientist 1 states in F, that comets are made of frozen materials anyway. It must be G (if comets were larger than 100 m diameter, the object couldn't be a comet).

Passage III

My 30-second look at the passage gets me the following information:

- H: Not sure exactly, but something to do with ants and elaiosome in seeds.

- Study 1 is just looking at the amount of elaiosome in seeds type A and B.

- Study 2 looks at whether ants take different amounts of seeds off different plants, depending on whether they do or don't grow locally (a little confusing initially – you should decide when you're reading whether to take the time to understand this).

- Study 3 looks at whether plants planted by ants do better than those planted by hand – they generally do.

- V: Seed type (A or B), how many seeds ants take if it's not a local plant, some other variables about the successes of different plants.

- C: You have to draw your own here, but Study 2 suggests that ants do take more seeds of a non-local plant, and that plants do better when grown by ant-planted seeds than hand-planted seeds. Again, you may not take the time to figure this out when you're reading the passage, that's fine.

13. A. The number of germinations in ant-planted seeds is about 50% higher (compare 26 and 39). There's no noticeable difference between seeds produced per plant after two years – the difference between the two numbers is 24, which is not a large difference compared to the 2000 or so seeds.

14. G. They placed two seed dishes in each site. The number of ants was not controlled, and the mass of elaiosome can't really be controlled! The type of seeds taken is the dependent variable here, so not the one that's controlled.

15. C. The percentages of elaiosome by mass are the same, as confirmed by Table 1.

16. G. F and H are not part of the experiment at all. J is probably the aim of the study overall – to see if ants prefer seeds with more elaiosome, but the question is asking specifically about site 3, which was the one with neither plant species A or B.

17. C. Read through these choices to see which one makes the most sense. A is part of the design of the experiment – they are trying to see if ants prefer the seed of non-local plants. B is not true – all three sites had seeds A and B. D doesn't make sense – the experimenters were not studying the plants, they were studying the seeds.

18. J. This is where it really pays off to have thought about the conclusion of the experiment! In Study 2, the ants took more of seed A when there were no A plants around, more of seed B when there were no B plants, and roughly equal amounts when there were no plants at all. This shows that ants have a preference for non-local seeds. Choice H doesn't work because the percentage of eliaosome is the same for A and B, and F and G don't work because the effect works both ways around – the ants take more A seeds under some conditions, and more B seeds under other conditions.

Passage IV

My 30-second look at the passage gets me the following information:

- H: Two different experiments measure the stickiness of different brands of tape to plastic and paper.

- V: Three brands were tested in a number of different widths.

- T: Wider tape always means better adhesion, generally brand Y appears best (compare all the average forces needed to remove tape with 2 cm width). Paper adhesion is usually better than plastic, except with brand Y. If you didn't get these last two points, that's OK, but you should have noticed that increased tape width means increased adhesion.

- A good thing to have noticed (but quite subtle) is that the tape widths used in Experiments 1 and 2 are the same for brands X and Y, but not for Z. This may make it difficult to draw conclusions about Z.

19. A. As observed above (bullet point 3).

20. G. Extrapolate the average values column for tape X. The column reads, 1.9, 3.9, 5.8. As tape width goes up by 1 cm, force goes up by about 2 N, so add 2 N to 5.8. The result is closer to 7 N than 9 N, so choose that.

21. A. Compare the average columns from Tables 1 and 2. The numbers for brand X are higher in Table 1; for brand Y, they are exactly the same. For Z, it's hard to tell because they tested a different tape width. All the answers say Y except for choice A, though.

22. G. Brand X had three widths in both experiments, Brand Z had two widths in Experiment 1, but only one width in Experiment 2.

23. A. The force between the clamp and the tape. Eliminate B and D because the objects mentioned are not in contact with each other! The tape is attached to the wrapping and the clamp, so when the force between clamp and tape is stronger than the wrapping and the tape, the tape will unstick from the wrapping.

24. F. For 2.5 cm tape, read between the second and third values in the average column of Table 1; 4.9 would fit there. Check against the Brand Y value for 2.5 cm tape, which is 5.4. Therefore, it's unlikely to be brand Y. If you're rushing, this is enough to get the answer, because all the choices include Brand Y except for F. If you have more time, you can confirm further using other values, but it's not really necessary.

Passage V

My 30-second look at the passage gets me the following information:

- H: The hypothesis is to do with factors affecting heat flow, from the first sentence.

- V: The variables are the material, distance between walls, configuration and initial temperature.

- T: You can pick out trends here, but given the way the data is organized, I decided not to. All your results are together in one column, which is not separated by any of the variables (e.g. one box for all the Configuration A results, or similar). This will mean that it will probably take a lot of time to find all the trends – easier to just pick them out in the questions. I did notice though, that there were some very high values for steel and aluminum, and I also noticed that in trials 1-6 with glass wool, the temperature change was always 30°C, no matter what the initial and final temperatures were.

- C: My observation above leads me to realize that the heat transfer rate isn't affected by the initial temperature.

25. B. You're looking for where T_2 is higher than T_1. That is only the case in Trial 6.

26. F. Look for the lowest heat flow. Obviously that's glass wool, but that's not an option. The next lowest heat flow is for wood.

27. D. See my fourth bullet point above, but if you didn't get that on your initial read, you can look at Trials 1 and 5, in which the configuration, material and heat transfer was the same, but the initial temperature was different. This tells you that initial temperature doesn't affect heat transfer rate.

28. H. The question is basically asking you to compare the heat flows for the different materials. Make sure you notice that it's a "NOT" question. Choice H is the only one that isn't true.

29. A. I started out by eliminating choices C and D, based on my answer to Q27 – I know that heat flow doesn't depend on initial or final temperatures. Also, those things don't vary between Trials 1 and 3. The difference between Trials 1 and 3 is the distance between the walls (configuration A versus configuration C).

Passage VI

My 30-second look at the passage gets me the following information:

- H: Hypothesis is to design an FRH, which works by the chemical equation given.

- V: In Experiment 1, the surface area of the magnesium was varied (powder vs. finely chopped ribbon vs. ribbon). In Experiment 2, varying amounts of Fe were added, and in Experiment 3, varying amounts of NaCl were added.

- T/C: Powdered magnesium produces the fastest rate of reaction, Fe increases the rate of reaction up to 0.5 mol, when adding more doesn't seem to matter. NaCl also increases the rate, but makes the solution boil after 0.125 mol.

30. H. If you didn't already spot this on your initial read, look back at Table 2 and note the asterisk, which gives you the answer.

31. A. If you put a trend arrow in Table 2, you'll already have seen that the values go up steadily as more NaCl is added.

32. G. 0.06 mol is right between two given values in Table 2 (0.05 mol and 0.07 mol), so interpolate between 34 and 50. The only answer between 34 and 50 is G.

33. D. You should have noticed that that was the key variable in experiment 1, but that Experiments 2 and 3 both used powdered magnesium.

34. F. You already know that powdered Mg is best, so cross off G and J. The difference between F and H is the concentration of Fe powder, but if you check Table 1, you'll see that there is no difference between the rate when 0.5 mol and 0.7 mol Fe is added. The question clearly states: "using the least amount of materials," so F is correct. If you didn't know how to choose between F and H, you should have realized you were missing some information, so read through the question again.

35. D. This is a tough one – it should be a skip question if you feel that you haven't understood the passage well! The question is telling you that the product $Mg(OH)_2$ forms a coating on the surface of the Mg reactant. You need to infer that this would slow the reaction, because reactions only happen on surfaces. You can also reason this out because you know that a greater surface area speeds up the reaction, from Experiment 1. Both B and C suggest a mechanism that would inhibit the reaction, which is the opposite of what NaCl actually does. A doesn't make much sense, because it says that NaCl absorbs heat, which then makes the $Mg(OH)_2$ melt. That is unlikely, because something that absorbs heat is likely to reduce the amount of melting, not increase it.

Passage VII

My 30-second look at the passage gets me the following information:

- H: The passage is about enzymes and factors affecting their acceleration factors.

- This is the kind of passage where your initial knowledge can make quite a big difference. Enzymes are a pretty standard biology topic, so this passage might be a breeze for you, or it might contain quite a lot of unfamiliar vocabulary. Choose your guess/skip questions accordingly.

- V: There are two enzymes tested, A and B. The pH and temperature are varied.

- T: There are four sets of data, which all compare the acceleration factor that enzymes A and B each cause under four different sets of conditions. It's probably not worth knowing much more than that right now.

- 36. F. Read the solid line in Figure 2 – the peak is at 5.

36. B. The two enzymes have the same rate where the lines on the graph intersect, which is between pH 6 and 7.

37. J. If the acceleration factor for B is dependent on both substrate and enzyme concentration, you would expect to see some variation in the graphs (i.e. not a straight horizontal line). There is variation, so the concentration depends on both.

38. A. Experiment 4 is about enzyme concentration, so rule out B and D. The graph shows that B is always lower than A under those conditions, so choose A.

39. G. First, use the information in the question to label the left curve stomach, and the right curve small intestine. Then, compared to the stomach, the small intestine curve is at higher pH values. You need to use your knowledge of the pH scale to understand that this means they're less acidic.

Practice test 2/Form 61C answer explanations

Passage I

My 30-second look at the passage gets me the following information:

- It's about plasmids and gene transfer. I spot that it's the conflicting viewpoints one.

- H: What order are the genes transferred in?

- C: The conclusions have to do with where the replication starts and what direction it goes in. I actually annotate the figure with some arrows and numbers to indicate what each student thinks.

1. B. In the third paragraph, it says that one gene is transferred every 15 minutes. After 50 minutes, that would be three and a bit genes, but the question asks for complete genes. Yes, you do have to do 50/3 without a calculator. If you think this is going to take you a while, write down 50/3 and put a star by the question so you can come back to it.

2. J. Student 3 thinks the replication goes clockwise from wherever it starts, so Gene 1 would be G, Gene 2 would be F and Gene 3 would be X.

3. C. Both their statements say: "Replication can begin between any two genes."

4. F. Student 1 thinks replication starts at X and goes clockwise. After 45 minutes, based on Q1, three genes would have been replicated. Based on student 1's proposed order, that's X, R and S, making Gene G the answer.

5. A. Student 2 thinks replication can go in either direction from the spot between F and X. That means after 30 minutes, the two replicated genes are either G and F or X and R. The only genes definitely not transcribed are A and S.

6. J. Students 1 and 2 state that Genes F and/or X have to be the last replicated, whereas students 3 and 4 are not specific about where the replication starts, meaning that A could be last according to their explanations.

7. D. Student 1 thinks that replication starts at Gene X and goes to R, then S, then A. If A is the last gene replicated, that's four genes. Four genes × 15 minutes gives 60 minutes.

Passage II

My 30-second look at the passage gets me the following information:

- Wow! This looks like a lot of information at first! From the first paragraph, I get that it's something to do with the moon Io, and that it's also about allotropes of sulfur (H).

- V: Every graph has reflectance on the y axis, and wavelength on the x axis, so that's really useful. Figure 1 identifies different allotropes of S, so I guess there will be some questions about identifying allotropes based on matching a line with a line in Figure 1.

- T: Reflectance is always higher at higher wavelengths for all the allotropes.

8. G. You need to look at Figure 1 for this, although it doesn't specifically say so. The lines for orange S, red S, brown S and white S all increase and never go downwards, while the line for SO_2 goes downwards after its initial upward curve.

9. C. You might need to read this more than once to get the meaning of the question, but it's basically telling you to look at Figure 3, and compare whether the large plumes are higher or lower than the small ones. The solid line (large) is always below the dotted one (small), so always lower. Get used to this type of phrasing if you found this question hard to interpret – the ACT uses it all the time.

10. H. From Figure 1, read upwards from 0.40 on the x axis. The corresponding y value is about 0.2.

11. D. You should be looking at the top graph in Figure 3 for the volcano Pele. That curve is most similar to Brown S. Check the numbers on the y axis to be sure.

12. H. The question is asking you to extrapolate the graph slightly beyond the given lines. Be careful to get the large and small plumes the right way around.

13. B. You should know from the graphs that the reflectance is different for different wavelengths, so it has to be either A or B. A 0.98 reflectance value most sensibly means 98% of light is reflected. Also, it's white S, and you might know that white is all colors of light reflected, so it makes more sense to choose a high number than a low number. Note that this isn't a knowledge question – but your knowledge might help you justify your answer.

Passage III

My 30-second look at the passage gets me the following information:

- It's a basic circuit experiment, in which three different studies were conducted.

- H: Something to do with the relationship between capacitance and resistance.

- V: In Study 1, it's the voltage across the capacitor over time. In Study 2, it's the time taken to reach 6 V at different capacitances. In Study 3, it's time taken to reach 6 V at different resistances.

- T: I've identified all the trends in the tables as direct trends (both increase or both decrease). There are no inverse trends.

14. F. You need to look at Table 1 and find the time taken to reach 7.6 V. 7.6 is lower than all the non-zero values listed in the table, so it must have happened within the first 12 seconds.

15. **C.** You need to look at Table 2, and think about where a capacitance value of 1.5 ($\times 10^{-6}$) would appear. The highest capacitance recorded is 1.2, so 1.5 would be above that. The trend in the right column is to go upwards as well, so choose a value higher than 8.3. To decide between 10.5 and 15, look at how the values are changing. As the capacitance doubles, the time also appears to double. That should make you expect a time of 16–17 seconds for a capacitance of 2.4. Your value should be in between those, so choose 10.5.

16. **J.** This is a great variables question. If you didn't identify the variables initially, just look in the headings of the tables – this experiment is testing how the resistance affects the time to reach a certain voltage. You can tell that the resistance is the independent variable because that is the one that the students are changing.

17. **A.** The voltmeter has to be connected across the resistor only. If you're not sure what the symbols mean, Figure 1 has labels. This is not a knowledge question, but knowing about circuit diagrams will help.

18. **F.** The question asks for the shortest amount of time, so look at Tables 2 and 3, and figure out whether it's the lowest or highest resistance/capacitance that gives the smallest time value. In both cases, it's the lowest value, so choose the option that has the lowest value for both.

19. **B.** This question has a lot of words, but basically it's asking, "Is it true that as capacitance increases, time taken to reach a given voltage increases?" If you are having trouble interpreting the question, cross out unnecessary words. It's describing what happened in Experiment 2, and you've probably already identified an increase-increase relationship there.

Passage IV

My 30-second look at the passage gets me the following information:

- H: This passage is about burning different substances in a bomb calorimeter.

- V: The amount of heat released is the dependent variable in all the studies. The independent variable is the substance.

- T: There's a trend in the amount of sucrose and heat released, and it's an increase-increase relationship.

20. **F.** This is really only about Table 2. The trend should be pretty easy to spot, even if you didn't get it in your initial look. Compare the two columns in Table 2 – as one increases, so does the other.

21. B. In Table 1, you can see that for all the pairs of values, as change in water temperature increases, so does heat released. There's no leveling off of values, so it has to be graph B.

22. G. Look at Table 2 and compare 0.5 g and 1 g – the heat released goes from 8 kJ to 1 6kJ. This is the same if you compare any other two values, and the question is asking what would happen for a decrease of one half.

23. A. Listing the values from Table 1 in order gives you potato, egg, bread, cheese. If you take the 1 g value for sucrose (16.0 kJ), you can see that it's more than bread, but less than cheese, hence A.

24. H. You really only need to use Table 1 for this, especially if you understood from Q22 that the relationship is perfectly linear. The experiment used 1 g of potato, which released 3.2 kJ of energy. If you used 5 g, that would be approximately 5 × as much, so choose 15 kJ.

Passage V

My 30-second look at the passage gets me the following information:

- H: This isn't really a hypothesis, but clearly the passage is about densities of different substances.

- V: Table 1 shows densities of different substances, some solids, liquids and gases. The two figures are both about water – liquid in Figure 1, solid in Figure 2.

25. D. This is a bit of a trick question. All you have to do is read the data from Figure 1, but it's asking you to read the graph backwards, that is, as the temperature decreases. So, reading backward, the graph increases then decreases.

26. G. Compare the top two boxes in the density column in Figure 1. The two highest numbers are 11.34 for solid lead and 13.59 for liquid mercury, meaning that the student is not correct in stating that a liquid will always have a lower density than a solid.

27. B. Figure 2 is a straight line that decreases with increasing temperature, therefore B is the only correct answer.

28. F. The heaviest (i.e. most dense, since all volumes are the same) liquid will be on the bottom. Comparing the density values tells you that mercury should be on the bottom, and ethyl ether on the top.

29. C. This is a rare ACT math question! Start by reading Figure 1 and finding that the density is 1 g/cm^3 at 4°C. This means that 1 g of water has a volume of 1 cm^3. Therefore, 100 g has a volume of 100 cm^3.

Passage VI

My 30-second look at the passage gets me the following information:

This is quite a complicated passage. There's a distinct hypothesis, four experiments (one of which had a result that's buried in the text of the passage), and lots of different numerical measures. For this reason, I've divided my explanation into two categories - stuff you should definitely notice, and stuff that it's good to know before you get to the questions, but not essential.

Essential things to notice:

- H: Researchers predicted that fragmentation would result in a decrease in animal populations and aboveground tree biomass (AGTB). This is right there in the second sentence. You should expect to see experiments about both quantities.

- V: The independent variable is the forest fragmentation, while the dependent variables are the AGTB and animal populations. Studies 1-3 measure the AGTB, and Study 4 measures the animal population.

- T: Studies 1, 3 and 4 show a strong correlation between the variables measured.

Good things to notice:

- T: Study 1 shows that the AGTB decreases most next to the areas where there is most deforestation. Be careful - the y axis is negative, which means that the largest decrease is found at the bottom of the axis. Study 2 is the same as Study 1, except that the regions studied were much further away from the deforested areas than in Study 1, and there was no measurable change in AGTB. Study 3 is again measuring similar data, but this time one side of the forest is adjacent to the deforestation. The percentage changes in the AGTB are greater than in Study 1.

- T: Study 4 shows changes animal populations near deforested areas. It's a long-term study that tracks populations over years, by seeing how many animals can be caught in an hour. The insectivore population suffers sharp decline in the two-year period following deforestation. The hummingbird population appears to increase slightly, and the frugivore population shows slight decline initially.

- C: The researcher's hypothesis is supported – there are definitely decreases in the AGTB near deforested areas, with the greatest decreases seen in regions closest to deforested areas. The only animal population that appears severely affected is insectivores.

30. F. The line in Figure 4 for frugivores decreases only.

31. D. The population of hummingbirds rises slightly, while the population of insectivores drops dramatically.

32. G. A value of 75 on the x axis (measuring distance from center of plot) corresponds to a value of -2.6 on the y axis.

33. C. Study 2 says the average change in AGTB was zero. This could happen if all the changes were zero, or if some of the changes were positive and a roughly equal amount of changes were negative.

34. J. The researchers hypothesized a decline in animal populations, but the hummingbird population shows an increase.

35. C. The given data is captured per 1000 hours, so if they worked for 10,000 hours total, you need to multiply the given number by 10. The year 2 value for insectivores is 80, so in fact they trapped 800 in total.

Passage VII

My 30-second look at the passage gets me the following information:

- H: It's about deposits left by glaciers.

- V: There's one of those cross-section graphs that's organized by depth, and it measures resistivity and CO_2. There's also a table that's organized by depth, too, and compares percentages of particles by size.

- T: There aren't big trends in the data, but the sand content does decrease with depth in the table.

36. H. The resistivity and CO_2 content of the given sample most closely matched Gray Till C.

37. D. For this question, you need to assume or know that the oldest glacial advances are the deepest. Therefore, the first/lowest layer deposited is Gray Till D.

38. G. The question is quite wordy, but it's asking you to compare the resistivity of sand a gravel to the till layers. The sand and gravel layers have a far higher resistivity than any of the till layers.

39. C. Bedrock has a resistivity of just below 40 ohms, which is closest to olive green and grey till.

40. J. The question again is quite wordy, but it's saying that current CO_2 deposits are much higher, and asking you to state what a higher value would be. The highest value in the table is 35, so choose greater than 35.

Practice test 3/Form 64E answer explanations

Passage I

There's a lot going on here! This is what I get from my initial look at the passage.

- H: It's to do with two different types of seismic wave – s and p waves.

- V: The two waves take different lengths of time to reach a seismograph, with s waves being slower.

- You should also notice the labels around the edge of Figure 1, which areas s and p waves hit. The scale on Figure 2 is on the right of the diagram, so you might miss it.

1. D. 125° is between 103° and 142°, which is the zone where neither p nor s waves arrive. It doesn't matter which side of the diagram you read from.

2. G. Follow one of the solid lines (representing p waves) through the core and the mantle. Some lines change direction, and some stop completely. The most accurate choice is that they enter the core and are refracted.

3. D. Extend the lines in Figure 3 and estimate their y axis values. I estimated 24 for the s wave and 12 for the p wave, giving a difference of more than ten minutes.

4. F. The "time the earthquake starts at the focus" is most reasonably interpreted as distance of 0 and time of 0.

5. A. Amplitude means the height of the waves (more accurately, distance from highest peak to lowest trough). The s waves are larger in amplitude than p waves, so choose A.

Passage II

Here's what I get from my 30-second initial look at the passage:

- H: The study seems to be measuring $\delta^{18}O$ values in different places across an area that used to be Lake Agassiz.

- V: Three different sites are used, and there are different soil conditions at each site, as illustrated by Figure 2.

- T: The graphs in Figure 3 show that for all three sites, lower $\delta^{18}O$ values seem to be associated with deeper areas in lake clay, but $\delta^{18}O$ values in glacial till are a bit higher.

6. F. The light grey area is thinnest on the left, representing Winnipeg.

7. C. Smaller $\delta^{18}O$ values are on the left of the graphs in Figure 3. The lowest values are all recorded between 20-30 m.

8. J. Moving from right towards Site 3 on the graph, you see the shaded area get smaller.

9. C. Look at the height of the glacial till layer (the middle layer). The highest point is Site 2, and the lowest is Site 3.

10. J. On all three graphs in Figure 3, the values for $\delta^{18}O$ at depth of 3 m are in the region of 18 to −14.

Passage III

My 30-second look at the passage gets me the following information:

- H: "The presence of bubble in cans of various liquids would affect the roll time."

- V: The students tested three different liquids in Experiment 1, different times between shaking in Experiment 2, and a half empty plastic can in Experiment 3. In Experiment 3, they didn't time the roll, but rather observed how long the bubbles lasted.

- T: Generally, the liquids roll more slowly after being shaken (from trials 2, 3, 4 and 5).

11. B. The aim of Experiment 3 is to observe how long it takes for the bubbles to disappear. This isn't possible with an aluminum can, hence they used a plastic one (it needs to be transparent).

12. J. Read the "before shaking" columns in Tables 1 and 2. Trials 1, 3 and 5 all have the same value.

13. D. In Experiment 2, the roll times are higher in the "after shaking" column than in the "before shaking" column.

14. H. The question doesn't tell you to look specifically at Experiment 3, but hopefully you've observed that this is the experiment that tells you how long the bubbles last. There is two

hours' difference between Trials 4 and 5 (i.e. Trial 5 happened two hours later), but the findings of Experiment 3 suggest that no bubbles remain after two hours.

15. A. Again, you need to look at Experiment 3, although it doesn't tell you to. No bubbles remain after two hours, so it's likely that the roll time would be the same as the roll time before shaking.

16. H. This is Experiment 3 again! It states that there are bubbles at 15 minutes, but not after two hours.

Passage IV

You may have studied this in school and be very confident with photosynthesis. If this is the case, then you can probably skip the passage and go straight to the questions. My initial look at the passage gets me the following information:

- H: It's about photosynthesis and its rate at different wavelengths.

- V: There are two graphs which both have an *x* axis of wavelength, but different *y* axes. Figure 1 displays the absorption of Chlorophylls a and b, whereas Figure 2 displays the rate of photosynthesis.

17. A. Follow the solid line in Figure 1. It has a peak at 470, which, according to Table 1, is blue light.

18. F. This is a knowledge question. If you are shaky on cell organelles, read up on them from page 52!

19. B. Look at Figure 2, and check each of the points to see if they are higher than the rate at 670 nm (which is about 90).

20. G. This is a knowledge one, too. You have to know that the process of photosynthesis forms glucose, which is a sugar.

21. C. The highest rate of photosynthesis is at 440 nm. According to Figure 1, this is also where chlorophyll a has the highest relative absorption.

Passage V

Here's what I notice from my initial look at the passage:

- H: The experiments are conducted to determine the density of common plastics.

- V: There are ten different liquids in Experiments 1 and 2, and 8 different plastics are also tested against these liquids in Experiment 3.

- T: This passage is great for identifying trends! The liquids are arranged in ascending order of density in both Tables 1 and 2, and in Table 3, there's a funny sort of diagonal trend if you follow the first R to appear in each row. This indicates that the plastics in Experiment 3 are also arranged in order of density.

- It's very useful to identify here that an S recorded in Table 3 indicates that the bead is more dense than the liquid, and an R means that the bead is less dense than the liquid.

22. G. This is referring to liquid 1, which is 100% ethanol (no water), so just take the value from the density column.

23. C. PA-11 is more dense than liquid 5 (the bead stayed), but less dense than liquid 6 (the bead rose). This puts it between 0.999 and 1.05.

24. H. 67.54 g would be the lowest value in Table 2, so the density must be more than 1.29. Each gap between mass values in Table 2 is about 3 g, and the corresponding density gaps are about 7 g/mL, so 1.35 is the best choice.

25. B. Liquid 4 is the most dense, and liquid 1 is the least dense, so it doesn't make sense for beads to rise in liquid 1 and rise in liquid 4. If they did this, they would have to be less dense than liquid 1, and more dense than liquid 4, which is impossible. An easier way of looking at it is that in all rows in Table 3, there are Ss before Rs, so B is the result that doesn't fit that pattern.

26. F. Taring is to do with weight (as it says in the second paragraph), so F is the only answer that refers to weight.

27. B. Polycarbonate is denser than liquid 8, but PA-6 is less dense than liquid 8. Therefore, polycarbonate is more dense than PA-6 (most dense to least dense is polycarbonate, liquid 8, PA-6). You can use process of elimination to get rid of C and D, which are factually wrong according to Table 3.

Passage VI

My initial look at the passage gets me the following information:

- H: The topic is two different fermentation pathways exhibited by bacteria.

- V: There are four different species of bacteria and two different broths in which they were tested. Experiment 1 looks simply at which type of fermentation happens for each bacteria in each broth, and Experiment 2 is a follow-up to decide whether an effect called synergism is happening. Don't worry about interpreting the experiment just yet, and don't worry if you don't understand what synergism is. You just need to know which experiment is about synergism.

28. H. Fermentation (either pathway) is represented by a + sign in the table. Both B and D have plus signs for the lactose broth.

29. C. To fill in the table for species B and C together, there should be plus signs wherever there are plus signs for B and C in Table 1.

30. G. Read each of the results in the question separately: if the bacteria produces neither acid nor CO_2 in sucrose, it can only be A or B. Then, if it produces both in lactose, it must be B.

31. D. For this question, you need to understand the definition of synergism. It means that the two bacteria together will make products that neither of them made alone. Look at Experiment 1 to find that neither C nor D can produce CO_2 when in lactose. The fact that they did in Experiment 2 is evidence of synergism.

32. G. Species D in the sucrose broth produced acid, which would make the pH lower, so yellow, but not CO_2, so no gas bubble.

33. D. Species A and C together produced both acid and CO_2 in the sucrose broth, but neither in the lactose broth. This is the same as species C in Experiment 1, so there is no evidence of synergism here.

Passage VII

This is the conflicting viewpoints passage. The scientists are debating whether genes are made of proteins or DNA. You should know that genes are made of DNA, but this passage is set in the 1940s, before that discovery! The passage tells you that DNA is made of nucleotides, while proteins are made of amino acids. Again, hopefully you should already know this, but don't assume too much about this passage, because there will be some statements made here that we now know are incorrect. The best way to approach this particular passage is more like the reading section. Instead of using HoVerCrafT, I've found the main evidence that's presented for each argument.

- The protein hypothesis says that genes are made of proteins, because DNA contains only four nucleotides, which wouldn't be enough information to make all the genes needed.

- The DNA hypothesis says that genes are made of DNA because the amount of DNA doesn't vary much in cells, but is half in egg and sperm (gametes), which makes sense. The amount of protein in a cell varies much more for different cell types.

34. H. The DNA hypothesis says that DNA is what chromosomes are made of, so more chromosomes should mean more DNA.

35. D. Amino acids and proteins are both found outside the nucleus, as stated in the second sentence of the DNA hypothesis, so you can rule these two out. Genes are known to be found in structures called chromosomes (second line of the passage), so if DNA is only in the nucleus, it must be because chromosomes are only in the nucleus.

36. J. The passage doesn't talk about protein in gametes, so not F. DNA is not found in the cytoplasm, so not G. DNA is also not composed of amino acids, so not H.

37. A. The protein hypothesis argues that DNA can't contain enough information with only four nucleotides. This is the principle objection.

38. F. Mitochondrial DNA would be outside the nucleus, so that contradicts the statement: "DNA is found exclusively in the cell's nucleus," in the DNA hypothesis.

39. B. The DNA hypothesis says that the amount of DNA in the cell is less variable than the amount of protein, which is evidence that it is the genetic material. So the best evidence against the protein hypothesis is that there are different amounts in different types of cell.

40. J. DNA is composed of nucleotides only, so J is the best answer.

Practice test 4/Form 67C answer explanations

Passage I

From my initial look at the passage, I get the following information:

- H: It's about beak depth of finches, which may be connected to whether or not the finches can get seeds of different sizes under different conditions.

- V: There are two types of finches in the study, and three different islands.

- T: In Study 2, the finches tend to have a deeper average beak depth in dry years.

1. D. The highest bar in both the middle and lower graphs of Figure 2 is around 10 mm.

2. J. In the description above Figure 3, it says that smaller seeds are more abundant in wetter

years. The only year labelled "wet" is 1984.

3. B. In Study 2, the researches were only looking at Island B. From Figure 2, you can see that on Island B, there are only *G. fortis* finches. Study 1 as a whole, though, considers Islands A and C, which have *G. fuliginosa* as well, hence B.

4. J. This answer is easiest to get by process of elimination. G doesn't make sense – there's no way that the average age of the finch population could be determined by beak depth. H doesn't make sense in terms of experimental practice – you wouldn't want to keep catching the same finches. This means the answer is J. (F is wrong because it's the overall aim of the experiment, not specifically the aim of tagging the birds. F is the choice you would pick if you were reading too quickly!)

5. C. First, look at Figure 3, at 1977. It's labelled as a dry year, and the description right above says that in dry years, the average size of seeds is larger, and refer back to the first paragraph to find out whether big or small beaks are better for big or small seeds (it's big beaks).

6. F. To find out what happens to *G. fortis* finches when they experience competition, look at the top and middle graphs of Figure 2. For Island A, *G. fortis* finches have an average beak depth of around 12 mm, whereas for Island B, *G. fortis* finches have an average of 10 mm beak depth.

Passage II

My initial look at the passage gets me the following information:

- H: It's to do with wet deposition of different ions in rain in different months.

- V: There are four different ions being measured across Studies 1 and 2, and in Study 3, the amounts of copper and zinc ions deposited is measured in rural and urban sites.

- T: There aren't many super obvious trends here, but generally the concentrations are low in July.

7. D. Read across the graphs in Figure 3. SO_4^{2-} is the only ion that has a maximum in February and a minimum in July.

8. G. Draw a line across the middle of the first graph in Figure 1. It should end up between 50 and 75 on the *y* axis.

9. A. Look at the third graph in Figure 3. It's lowest for April to October, and higher in the other months.

10. H. Read back to the first sentence of the passage. Wet deposition is deposited ions from precipitation. Therefore, there can be no wet deposition if there is no rain. Also, all the values of the deposited ions drop in July, when there is less rain.

11. C. Look at the description for Study 3. Rural site 2 is further away from the urban site, so for both ions, there is a downward trend as you move away from the urban site.

12. F. In Study 2, Cl⁻ and SO_4^{2-} are being measured, and monthly rainfall can't be kept constant, so it must be the site.

Passage III

My initial look at the passage gets me the following information:

- H: The second sentence is your hypothesis: "Cloud cover may increase because of an increase in the cosmic ray flux."

- V: Table 1 shows how cosmic ray flux varies with cover of low clouds. The three graphs show cosmic ray flux over time, at three different cloud levels.

- T: In Table 1, you can see that cosmic ray flux increases with percentage cover of low clouds. You can also see that the RCRF lines don't follow cloud cover much, except in Figure 3, where the two are well correlated.

13. B. Read the dashed line from Figure 1 for 1983. It's closest to 13.5%.

14. H. Extrapolate Table 1 by adding an extra value. 440,000 would be the next value in the table, and it follows the pattern of a 20,000 gap between values. The gap between values in the second column is about 0.3%, so choose 29.3%.

15. A. You've already spotted this if you've found the same trends as I have in my initial look.

16. G. Be careful here! First, remember to read the dashed lines from the graphs, as these represent cloud cover. Also ensure that you read off the left-hand y axis, not the right-hand one. The value for high clouds in January 1992 is 13.5%, the value for middle clouds is about 22% and the value for low clouds is about 28%.

17. D. This is basically logical. We know that for ice to form, the temperature must be around 0°C or below. According to the question, this will happen at high altitudes. Ensure that you choose the choice that reads 6–16, which is defined in the passage as high clouds.

Passage IV

This is a titration passage. If you feel comfortable with titrations, you could probably save time by going straight to the questions here. If you're not sure what's going on, spend a little more time reading the passage. Since titration is a common technique, it's worth knowing about it. I've written about it in the chemistry section of this book, so make sure you read through that, too.

For this passage, here's what you should notice:

- H: The titration is being measured in two ways: by conductivity, and by use of an indicator. You should expect some questions comparing the two methods.

- V: In Experiment 1, HCl is the acid used. In Experiment 2, it's acetic acid.

- T: In Experiment 1, the conductivity falls and then rises, whereas in Experiment 2, it rises only.

18. F. The narrow dotted line (the first part) of Figure 1 shows you where the solution was yellow. Any answer between 0-1 mL would be acceptable.

19. B. The last part of the introduction tells you the color of nitrazine yellow. You can infer that green is the color for pH 6-7 from what's written. You need to know that pH 7 is neutral. In Figure 2, the color of the solution is green at around 1 mL of titrant.

20. J. Extend the line on Figure 1 - you will find that it rises above 3.8 kS/cm.

21. C. You have to do a lot of reading around to answer this question. From the first paragraph, find that the titrant is the one added. From the introduction of Experiment 1, find that that is the NaOH. From the introduction to Experiment 2, find that acetic acid was used.

22. J. In Experiment 1, it tells you that the probe measures conductivity. This would most logically be done by passing a current through the solution.

23. A. The pH at 0.2 mL of titrant is low, as the indicator is yellow. The pH at 1.8 mL is high, as the indicator is blue. So, no, the chemist's hypothesis is not supported.

Passage V

This is the conflicting viewpoints passage, so remember that you're mostly looking for hypotheses and conclusions. However, this one seems a little different to the typical set-up. You're given some facts, then statements from two students about stars in the Algol system, which contains three stars. I would expect the questions to be asking you to test the facts against the students' statements, so I wouldn't read too closely before going to the questions here.

24. H. Student 2's discussion doesn't say specifically why Algol B became part of the system, but you should link it with the mention of gravity in Fact 2. If this seems tenuous, you could also view this as a knowledge question – you might already know that objects in space orbit each other because of gravitational attraction.

25. B. This question seems really complicated, but all you need to do is take the phrase from Fact 4 and select the closest answer. You also need to know that Algol B is a post-MS star at this point, in order to figure out that Fact 4 is applicable here (but the question tells you to use Fact 4 anyway).

26. G. Student 2's argument is that Algol A and C are the original system, and B drifts in later. This would make the most similar two stars A and C.

27. C. In the paragraph following the facts, it states that the mass of Algol C is 1.7 × the mass of the sun, so you need to multiply 1.7 by 2×10^{30}.

28. G. This is a knowledge question. You must know that protons are positively charged and that like chargers repel each other. Heat and pressure are necessary to overcome this and fuse the nuclei together, but in fact, the question can be answered just by selecting the correct fact.

29. B. Student 1 says Algol B is initially the most massive star, and Fact 5 says that the more massive a star, the faster it progresses through stellar evolution.

30. H. This is a pretty tricky question because of the wording. If you're ever unsure of what the question is asking, see if you can eliminate some of the answers. Here, you can eliminate G and J because they claim that Algol A has always been smaller than B, whereas in the passage, it's the other way around. Be careful though – they change around the wording between the passage and the question, so you could be tempted to choose the wrong one. For the other part of the question, the answer is "no." If the two stars are different masses, according to Fact 5, they will progress at different speeds through the stages of stellar evolution.

Passage VI

My initial look at the passage gets me the following information:

- H: Having read through the passage, it seems to be something to do with weighing three different gases.

- T: As mass of gas increases, pressure increases. You would expect this logically anyway. The difference between Figures 1 and 2 is the size of the vessel. The trend is the same for both vessels, but the scale is slightly different. Again, that's entirely logical.

31. C. Extrapolate the lowest line on Figure 2.

32. G. Read between the two values for CO_2 on each graph. On Figure 1, 7 g gas gives 1000 Torr, whereas on Figure 2, 7 g gas gives 500 Torr.

33. A. You can answer this based on your reasoning from the previous question, as the trends are the same for all the gases. The pressure is lower in the 6 L vessel (because the gas has more room to spread out), and it's roughly by a factor of 2, in other words, half as great.

34. J. You can read the graphs to get the lesser/greater part of the question. All the O_2 lines are above the CO_2 lines, meaning O_2 exerts greater pressure. The reason for this is because O_2 (two atoms) is a smaller molecule than CO_2 (three atoms), 1 gram of O_2 will contain more molecules.

35. A. This is really a knowledge question. Lowering the pressure of a gas will lower its temperature because of the Gay-Lussac law, which states that pressure of a gas is directly proportional to its temperature – in other words, if one falls, the other must fall too.

Passage VII

My initial look at the passage gets me the following information:

- H: This data is presenting information about sound, threshold of hearing and threshold of pain. It also displays a quantity, S. Don't worry if you don't really understand what S is. When you look at the information, you should realize that you have a definition of S, and that it's also on the graph. Beyond that, it doesn't matter.

- V: The graph displays frequency vs. intensity.

36. G. Follow the line for "threshold of hearing" down to its lowest point. That's around 2×10^1 Hz, that is, 20 Hz.

37. A. If hearing loss occurs at higher frequencies, you should expect the line for threshold of hearing to get lower. This happens in graph A.

38. F. This is a tough one! The question says "at a given frequency." This means read across from the y axis. The water lines are always higher intensity than the air ones, so you can rule out H and J. The highest intensity line is at S = 100%.

39. C. This is a real trick one, and I don't like it! First, use process of elimination to get rid of B. B is not true – threshold of pain doesn't increase after 10^5 Hz, we know nothing about frequencies higher than 10^5 Hz because the graph doesn't go that high. The statement contained in A and D is true, but it isn't the answer. The phrasing of the question says "painful for humans to hear." The threshold of hearing doesn't go up to 10^5 Hz, so even if it were painful, we wouldn't hear it. I prefer choice D personally, but because of the phrase "to hear," the answer has to be C.

40. J. There are a number of different S lines, but they don't change with intensity.

Practice test 5/Form 1572-CPRE answer explanations

Passage I

My 30-second look at the passage gets me the following information:

- H: The passage is something to do with two different strains of fruit flies and their life span.

- V: In Study 1, the experimenters use 15% SY medium, whereas in Study 2 they use 5%. There are three different types of media in each study. In Study 3, the experimenters compare the two strains, X and N under different conditions.

- T: In Table 1, you can observe that for both X and N strains, as the percentage of sugar and percentage of yeast go up, the life span goes down.

1. C. You're looking for any point in graphs 1 and 2 where there are still some fruit flies left after 75 days. The only situation where this happens is in Graph 2, for the 5% SY medium and nothing else.

2. G. If the population is decreasing, it can't be because the death rate is zero – that doesn't make sense. So it must be F or G. Check back at the description of the studies and you'll find that they only used female flies.

3. D. If you read the "Key" box for each of the studies you will see that the difference is 15% SY medium in Study 1 and 5% SY medium in Study 2.

4. G. The question wants you to look at Strain X, so make sure you're looking at the bottom half of the table first. It would like to know the lifespan for flies exposed to a 12% sugar medium, so choose a value between the 10% and 15% that you're given, that is, a lifespan of 55.6-58.6 days.

5. C. The prediction is correct, because Strain X flies (with less sense of smell) live longer than Strain N flies (N is normal). Compare the last column of Table 1 to find this information.

6. F. If the researchers want to know something about 15% SY medium, they need to repeat Study 1. The odor defect is Strain X flies, and Strain N was what was originally used in Study 1 anyway.

7. A. The absence of live odors and live yeast would be the first of each set of tubes from Studies 1 and 2. In the descriptions for each of the studies, it says that tubes 1 and 4 contained no additional substances, so you want to compare these two tubes. Comparing the calories would best be done by comparing Studies 1 and 2 because they have different amounts of sugar.

Passage II

This is the conflicting viewpoints passage, so, as usual, there are multiple hypotheses. This passage actually labels them as hypotheses, so that should really jog your memory to use HoVerCrafT!

The hypotheses are to do with when monarch butterflies store and use energy during their migration and overwintering period. There are two ways to approach this passage.

If you just need a very brief overview before moving to the questions, it should be sufficient to know that the hypotheses are all debating about when monarch butterflies store and use energy during their migration and overwintering period.

If you're someone who likes to really understand the passage before you go to the question, you can make this little table, like I did:

	Before Migration	During Migration	Overwintering
H1	Store	Uses	Uses
H2	Store	Uses	—
H3	—	Store	Uses

8. F. Hypothesis 1 says that lipids must be stored both before migration and before overwintering. Hypothesis 2 says that lipids must only be stored before migration, and Hypothesis 3 says that they are only stored during migration.

9. D. See previous answer explanation – all of the hypotheses state that lipids are used in either migration or overwintering.

10. J. Ensure that you read the bit in brackets first – the period described by the graph ends at

the end of migration. Hypothesis 3 states that energy is stored during migration and is used in the overwintering period, but the graph does not include the overwintering period. This means that the energy should only increase, not increase and then decrease, thus J is the correct graph.

11. C. This is a complicated question to understand, but it's basically asking which of the hypotheses say that the butterflies have more stored lipids at the beginning. This is 1 and 2 because those both claim that lipid supplies are used during migration.

12. F. Hypothesis 1 is the only one that states that the butterflies need to store lipids directly before overwintering, hence that they would need nectar at the overwintering sites.

13. B. The hypotheses don't agree on much, but B is the least specific choice! Hypotheses 1 and 2 state that stored lipids decrease during migration, whereas Hypothesis 3 states that stored lipids increase during migration, so B reflects that.

14. F. This is a rare knowledge question! Starch results from joining together sugar molecules, amino acids are the constituents of proteins, and DNA is the molecules forming the genetic code. ATP is the cell's equivalent of fuel.

Passage III

My initial look at the passage gets me the following information:

- H: I didn't really bother reading the introductory paragraph. It's something to do with greenhouse gases, but that's all I need to know.

- V: I see that both Figure 1 and Figure 2 have exactly the same axes, and both are displaying CH_4 concentration and solar radiation. These two things appear to move together, except in the last half of Figure 2, where solar radiation drops but CH_4 concentration rises. I also notice that Figure 2 is showing more recent data than Figure 1.

15. C. This is just reading the graph. Follow the dashed line for solar radiation intensity, be careful to read off the left-hand y axis.

16. F. If the CH_4 concentration trend matches the solar radiation trend, you can just read a value from the solar radiation line. This would be approximately 450 ppb, as the line dips down. Read from the right-hand y axis because it's asking you to give a figure for CH_4 concentration.

17. B. This question is very wordy, but it's essentially asking you to give the general shape of the

trend in CH_4 concentration. This is the solid line from Figure 2, which most closely matches with graph B.

18. H. If you drew a line through the middle of the graph in Figure 1, it would fall at approximately 480 watts/m^2.

19. B. This is asking for the distance between peaks for the dashed line in Figure 1. Check for more than one set of peaks, but this corresponds to an interval of about 20 on the x axis of the graph. This is measured in thousands of years, so 20,000 is an appropriate value.

20. J. This is partly a knowledge question. The first sentence of the passage tells you that greenhouse gases warm the climate, so you should not choose F or H. You then have to know that J is a much more plausible explanation than G. Choice G is suggesting that giving out UV energy would make something warmer, which is not true.

Passage IV

My initial look at the passage gets me the following information:

- H: The students are measuring the force needed to pull a block along a surface.

- V: In Experiment 1, they measure the force for different masses. In Experiment 2, they measure the speed that three blocks of different mass obtain when pulled by a constant 30 N force.

21. D. You have to know that frictional forces oppose the direction of motion, so if the pulling force is east, the frictional force will be acting to the west.

22. F. Find 15 m/s on the y axis of Figure 2, and draw vertical lines from where each line has a y value of 15. The first line you draw will be for the 2 kg block.

23. B. Acceleration is the rate of change of velocity, or the slope of the line in the graph. You need to do a quick rise over run calculation for the 3 kg block, which gives you $15 \div 3$, which is 5.

24. J. Again, treat this like a math question. Pulling force is on the y axis, and block mass is on the x axis, so you should not choose F or G. If you take any of the x values from Figure 1, you will see that you need to multiply them by 5 to get the y values, so following a typical linear equation construction, the slope is 5.

25. B. Heavier blocks were slower, which is what you should expect anyway, so as block mass increases, block speed decreases.

26. H. Extend the line in Figure 1. You should expect a value of around 6 N, but if you need further confirmation, you can be sneaky and use your answer to Q24 to find the equation!

Passage V

My initial look at the passage gets me the following information:

- H: It's about acid base indicators. This is great if you know about this topic. If you don't, go back and read my section on it (page 47) – it comes up often enough that it's worth knowing!

- I notice that Experiments 1 and 2 are basically the same, but in the two different halves of the pH scale.

- V: The variable is the indicator that they are testing. This is a strange one for trends, but I circled the point at which each of the indicators changes color to make it easier to find this later. Experiment 3 is unknown solutions, so their pH could be identified by comparing with Experiments 1 and 2.

- A great tip for this particular passage is to notice that the indicators are in the same order in all the tables, so if you are trying to match an unknown solution from Experiment 3, you can read the column and simply match the column to one in Table 1 or 2 to determine pH.

27. A. You have to choose the thing that is true for Experiment 2 but not 3. Cross off C and D, as metanil yellow was used in both. It was only in Experiment 3 that the pH was unknown, but choice A is the opposite – known pH in Experiment 2.

28. J. This is an experimental reasoning question. If you're trying to determine the color of liquid solutions, the best background for that is white. I found the phrasing of the question a bit strange and had to read it twice, but this is the reason they're looking for.

29. C. Curcumin is yellow at pH 7, orange at pH 8 and red at pH 9. This suggests its transition point is around 8, so choose an interval that has 8 as its center.

30. F. If you don't understand the question, you can simply check which statements are true. Indigo carmine is blue at both pH 1 and 6, so it must be F or H. Now you must reason that in order to tell the difference between a pH 1 and 6 solution, the indicator cannot be the same color at both pHs, hence the answer is F.

31. B. Look for an indicator that has a transition point around 5.

32. G. For solution 3, metanil yellow is yellow, indicating a pH of 3 or greater, but resorcin blue is red, which suggests less than 5, so it cannot have a pH of 7.3.

33. D. I saved myself time by realizing that metanil yellow is the best one to detect low pH. Solution IV is the only one where metanil yellow isn't yellow, suggesting a pH of 2.

Passage VI

My initial look at the passage gets me the following information:

- H: The passage is about how drilling mud affects albedo and soil temperature.

- V: There are three plots in the study with different amounts of DM, and the experimenters measured albedo and soil temperature on each plot during July and August.

34. J. This is just logic. The sunlight at noon (12 pm) is greatest – the sun is hottest in the middle of the day.

35. A. This is basically asking you what the independent variable is in this experiment. The answer is drilling mud – this is the one that they were looking to investigate the effect of.

36. H. The question is telling you that rain decreases albedo measurements on the day afterwards. You need to look for a day that has a drop in albedo, and select the day before. The graph in Figure 1 drops on July 27th, so you can infer that it rained on July 26th.

37. B. This is such a sneaky one! In the last paragraph (top of the second column) it tells you that measurements were taken every five seconds, but the question asks you how many per minute. You need to do 60 ÷ 5 to get 12.

38. F. In the middle of the fifth paragraph it tells you that albedo measurements were only recorded on cloudless days. You can see from Figure 1 that no measurement was taken on 20 July. This means it was cloudy.

39. D. Plot 3 has the most DM, and the lowest albedo, meaning that DM decreases albedo. Plot 3 also has the highest soil temperature, meaning that DM likely increases soil temperature.

40. J. On August 3rd, the albedo is 0.2. From the definition in the second paragraph, you can see that albedo is the portion of radiation that's reflected. You need the portion not reflected, so choose 80%.

Useful Things Appendix

The purpose of this appendix is to help answer your questions about the ACT and related issues. This book only aims to tackle the Scientific Reasoning section, but of course there are a whole host of other questions that can factor into decisions you make when you're working through this book. For example, if you are really struggling to complete the ACT reading section in time, and are wondering if you should switch to the SAT because you've heard it has a more generous time limit, you really need to answer that question before you waste time preparing for the ACT! You might not know what your scores mean in terms of what universities you would like to apply to, which is also important. If your ACT score is already above the average for the schools you are applying to, it might not be worth spending more time preparing!

If you are located in the USA, you should contact your college counselor for advice that's specific to you. Someone who has your transcript in front of you and already knows you will be much more useful than general advice in a book! However, if you don't have access to a college counselor, or are an international student, I hope I can point you in the right direction.

If you're looking for a source of general information or a place to contact me directly, you should visit my website, prepACTSAT.com. Some of the questions I answer here are discussed more fully in articles there, and, of course, I am updating it all the time.

Two questions that I get asked all the time that I won't answer:

- Is a 25 a good score? I won't answer this, because it depends entirely on what you want to do with it. "Good" means literally nothing in reference to an ACT score – it's all relative to what you want to do with it. You should only be comparing your ACT score to one other ACT score, and that is the average score of admitted students at the school(s) you want to go to. Most people ask this question because they want to compare with their friends, or Bill Gates, or their mum or someone else completely irrelevant!

- Will I get into [insert school name]? I have no idea! First, I do not deal with admissions, and even if I did, I could not answer that question. Whether or not you get into any school depends on that school and what balance of test score/GPA/personal factors they are looking for. Every school is different, and every student is different. People ask this question because they want someone to reassure them. No one can do that. You either will get in or you won't and you won't know until that letter is in your mailbox (or digital equivalent!). If you're looking to make a shortlist of schools that are realistic for you to apply to, that's a great question! I answer it below.

Where can I find more tests?

In this book, I've directed you to use two of the free tests that the ACT publishes on their website. There are three more, and I've got full answer explanations to all five of these tests, starting on page 80. However, every student should practice with more than just these. My recommendation would be to buy a practice book. Most ACT practice books are good quality, since the test has been around in its current format for quite a while. Don't do tests from a computer screen – you will be writing a paper test, and annotation skills (i.e. HoVerCrafT) are key for the scientific reasoning section. If you are worried about wasting paper, print two pages per sheet if your eyesight is good, and recycle the paper when you are finished with the test.

I won't recommend any specific books for you here, but just go to any popular book-selling website and read the reviews. These should be a good guide for what other people have found helpful.

How should I practice for the other sections on the ACT?

Generally, your practice method should be similar to what I've outlined here for the scientific reasoning. Make sure you understand what the section is testing, break it down into small, untimed chunks, then gradually work up to doing a full section in the given time limit. And the key – make sure you review all your mistakes and understand them. I know I've said this already throughout the book, but just in case you landed in this section first, if I had a mantra for the ACT, it would be this: *If you don't take the time to understand your mistakes, you will only repeat them!* It will take you five times as long to improve your score because you're not actually learning from your mistakes, you're just repeating them. Work smart, not hard. (Sometimes you have to work hard, but other times you can avoid it!)

For the English and Math sections, it's important to make sure you have a strong knowledge foundation first. For English, this doesn't have to be extensive – a quick review of grammar and punctuation rules should suffice. For math, depending on your background and how intensive your courses have been to date, you may not need much more in the way of topic review. It's also important to remember not to freak yourself out about math. A lot of the topics tested are quite basic, so if your curriculum has been rigorous in emphasizing problem-solving skills, that will serve you better than knowing loads of calculus (there's none of that on the test!). I have a good concise topic list on my site at http://prepactsat.com/what-exactly-is-on-the-act-math.

How do I know what score I need to get?

When you first start thinking about university, you may not have much of an idea of where you want to go. This will make it difficult to determine what score you need to get on the ACT. First of all, most students do not need to begin making a university shortlist until the summer before their second to last (11th grade, or junior year). This may be different under special circumstances if you are looking to get an athletic scholarship, or you're studying something creative that requires you to have a portfolio. If this is the case, then you should be getting specialist advice anyway.

Second, get specialist advice! There are lots of factors that go into choosing the right university for you, especially in the USA. If you are an international student reading this, be aware that there are many different types of universities in the USA. A university will select you based broadly on three factors – your high school grades, which are a predictor of your desire and drive to learn, your ACT/SAT score, which is a reflection of your learning skills and aptitudes, and personal factors such as your essays, extracurricular activities, passions and interests, and the overall picture of you as a student. The balance of these three factors differs widely between universities: for some, the personal factors are most important, for others, academic profile may be enough on its own. The most selective schools will choose applicants who present strongly in all three areas, and even stand out from the other applicants. Some schools are test optional, which means that you don't have to write the SAT or the ACT at all for them (find them at fairtest.org). Some universities have a certain ethos or philosophy, such as strongly recommending a study abroad year, mandatory courses in what they consider to be core subjects such as philosophy, math or writing, some have religious affiliation, some make great effort to keep class sizes small, some make a particular point of their technology based learning ... you get the picture. Almost every type of learning environment and learning philosophy can be found at an American university. Many students from other countries don't fully appreciate the diversity in style that can be found in the USA. This is why there is such a wide choice of universities available, and this is why you should absolutely get professional advice if reading this makes you even more confused than before! Consider starting here to find a professional: www.hecaonline.org or nacacnet.org/membership/member-directory.

If you have some schools in mind, and you want to know roughly what score you'd need for them, almost all schools publish their admission statistics: GPA, ACT/SAT score, etc. If your profile looks similar to the students they admitted then that school would be a good one to put on your list. Just search "class of 2020 [school name] admissions profile." Remember to be realistic in where you apply. There is nothing wrong with applying to one or two schools that you may not get into, but you should always apply to at least two schools that have admissions profiles that match yours. What I mean by this is that if your GPA is a 3.5 and your ACT score is a 27, at least two of your schools need to have average ACT scores at or below a 27, and average GPAs of 3.5 or below.

A tally chart of "why I made my mistakes"

A few times in this book I have suggested that you compile a tally chart of why you made mistakes, in order to help you to improve. If you don't know what I mean, or are struggling to think of suggestions, here's what I mean. You can use this one as a template. Try to be as specific as possible – you need to use this so that you can improve in the future. Remember not to take this negatively, learn from it!

Reason	Number of mistakes
Distracted	IIII I
Read the wrong graph	III
Didn't understand the question	I
Ran out of time	
Didn't understand the passage	II
Didn't see a piece of information I needed	IIII III
Wasn't sure which information to use	II

The ACT answer sheet (bubble sheet)

Before you write the test for real, make sure you've practiced a full test at least once, using the official ACT bubble sheet (also known as an answer sheet). It's one less thing to worry about on test day. You can find one at the end of all the official ACT practice tests. I have some pretty specific recommendations about when to fill this in. I've written about it in "Bringing it all Together," but I'll say it again here too: The most efficient way to fill in the bubble sheet is after every passage. This way, you don't have to think about it when you're actually answering the questions, but you're not leaving it until the end of the test either. It means you won't run out of time filling it in at the end of the test, and you won't waste time by finding your place on it throughout the test. This will work for Scientific Reasoning, English and Reading, because each of these is split into passages. For Math, choose a point in the test that you can guarantee you'll get to before the five-minute warning, and make that your bubble point. For most students, I'd suggest bubbling after question 30, then again at question 50 or the five-minute warning (whichever is first), then fill in the bubbles as you complete each question.

Should I write the SAT instead?

Some people start out writing one test, then switch to the other during their prep. Other people start by choosing one or the other and sticking to it. Some students even write one test, then give the other a shot just to see. If you think the ACT isn't working for you, the SAT is something to consider. First of all it's important to note that no matter what you might have heard, the tests are equivalent, that is, all schools accept both. Anyone who says otherwise doesn't know what they're talking about. It used to be believed that there was a geographic bias towards the SAT or ACT, but that is no longer true. It's also important to know that most students perform similarly on the tests. The tests really are quite similar. Whether you should make the switch or not is quite an individual decision, so here are the factors that you should consider.

Things that are common to both tests:

- Five sections, including an optional essay

- Vocabulary is only tested in context

- Total test time is about three and a half hours

- The ACT English and the SAT Writing and Language sections are virtually identical

The ACT...	The SAT...
Has a scientific reasoning section! Hopefully you've realized this if you're reading this book!	Has a data based component, but this is assessed from the Reading and Math sections (plus a little bit on the writing and language).
More extensive documentation needed to get accommodations such as extra time.	Accommodations can often be approved automatically based on what you get in school.
Has one math section, representing a quarter of your score. Calculator allowed.	Has two math sections, representing half your score. Calculator only allowed on one of the two sections.
Essay is discussion or opinion based.	Essay is analytical.
Timing is key on Reading and Scientific Reasoning.	Much more generous time limit on Reading, but some of the passages can use difficult, old-fashioned language.
Math questions are usually more straightforward in wording, but can test more advanced content	Math is wordy and requires lots of interpretation.
Wider variety of topics on math.	Lots of linear systems and data based reasoning in math.

Lots of past tests available, good quality practice that's realistic to the test.	Only seven tests available, approximately three added per year. Books are less representative of the test than they are for the ACT. There aren't as many SAT books to study from.

Once you've read over this table, see which test you gravitate towards. If math is a strength for you, but you struggle to read quickly, then try the SAT. If you're about the same on both tests, but you are aiming for a very high score (or a score that is much higher than what you have now), you may want to choose the ACT, as there's more practice material available.

What's the best way for me to prepare?

There are a number of different methods that people use to prepare for the ACT. If you're reading this, you've already chosen to use books as part of your prep method. Other things you might want to consider are online programs, group courses and private tutoring.

There are four main factors you should consider: the time you have to prepare, the amount of money you can spend, your own self-discipline and what your goal is. The balance of these factors should tell you the best method for you.

Important facts to bear in mind:

- No method is going to produce results instantly.

- The more tailored your program is, the quicker you should see results.

- You need time to practice. Four months or more is ideal. Two weeks is not enough.

- Be realistic about your target score.

- Most of your improvement will depend on you – all methods require you to do some independent study.

If you know you're pretty motivated, and you won't have trouble committing to four hours' work per week when you're not accountable to anyone for it, then you might be able to do your prep on your own with books and the Internet to help guide you. Helpful supplements to this method include being accountable to someone else – agree to do the same amount of work as a friend, ask a family member to remind you to study, etc. If you have less than three weeks to prepare, or if your target score is more than ten points away on the ACT, you'll find it hard to hone your skills that much by yourself in a short time. If you are currently scoring below a 21, then you may also find it hard to improve on your own.

You may want to consider a private tutor if you feel that you need individualized preparation, or have only a very short time. This is probably the most expensive way to prepare, with prices ranging between $70-600 per hour. Look for someone with experience, and get recommendations from friends and family. If you are towards the higher end of the scoring range and want a cheaper option, someone who has taken the test before and got a high score may be able to help you. The lower your score is, the more likely you are to need more general advice than specific questions, so it's more important to have an experienced tutor. Good tutors can survive solely on word of mouth recommendations. A tutor is best if you haven't got long to prep – they can show you the areas you need to work on most quickly and can more quickly find resources that are most suited to your needs. A tutor is probably the best way to improve your score by a large margin (e.g. more than eight points). I would also use a tutor if you are scoring under 21 on the ACT. In this score range, you'll have a tough time assessing your weaknesses on your own, and a group course could be pitched at a higher scoring range than what you are working towards. You may have a specific weakness in one area (e.g. reading), so a tutor can help you with that outside of the test as well. If you're struggling with motivation, a tutor can hold you accountable for doing your work too!

Group prep courses are a great way to get a general introduction to the test. There are some big name companies which many people find helpful. As always, research the program before you sign up. Remember that to get the best out of it, you still need to practice and prepare on your own.

There are also many online prep courses. I think these courses are good for the motivated student, and also you should probably treat them like group courses. They should be part of your prep program, not the only thing you use to prepare. When you're choosing a course, make sure you know exactly what you're signing up for (including whether there is a refund period). Get a recommendation from a friend, or look for online reviews that prove that the program gets results. There are some companies that have fancy marketing but poorly designed programs, which don't reflect the tests at all. Also make sure that they do what they say they do in terms of personalizing your program to you: some companies say they will do this, but don't. Beware of companies that promise you a score improvement (unless they are using that promise as a money-back guarantee).

One thing to be aware of is apps and online tools that emphasize preparing by doing single questions. There is nothing wrong with this in principle, and it's a great way to do a little bit of test prep, but it cannot replace sitting down and doing a full section of the test! It's all very well if you can answer the Question of the Day every day, but if you can't concentrate for 3.5 hours, you will struggle with the test. In my experience, this is a factor for about 50% of students, so make sure that you've addressed this. Online programs can be particularly bad for these, especially ones that are based around an app. This is a great catch to get you, a teenager, into their product, but make sure that this is only a supplement to you sitting down in a quiet room and doing some old-school pencil and paper studying. Think of it this way: you won't get fit by running 10 meters and doing a single push up per day. That might be a good place to start, but you must progress from there!

When should I be writing the ACT?

For most students, the second to last year of high school (11th grade/junior year) is their ACT year. Taking it much earlier than that is not usually necessary. If you're in 10th grade and think you can do well, by all means try it, but bear in mind that you'll likely do better with an extra year of education. Any earlier than 10th grade is usually pointless. There are one or two gifted programs that ask for the ACT taken in 8th grade as an entry requirement. If you want to do that, go ahead. But if you are looking for a score to get you into university, I would not recommend starting earlier than your 10th grade year.

Start your prep in the summer before your 11th grade, and continue it through the fall. For the ACT, the December test is usually a good first test to attempt. You can get the test paper back by applying for Test Information Release (available in December, April and June), and there's enough of a gap that you can look and learn from it by the February test. At the beginning of 12th grade, it may be a good time to revisit the ACT and see whether you can improve your score. Some students find that their score will improve by the end of 11th grade, so if you are applying for competitive schools, or you didn't quite get the ACT score you wanted before, then this may be a good idea. Remember that the test is skill based, not knowledge based. What you do in the week before the ACT matters very little. It's how you build your skills in the months leading up to the test. This is one of the most important things to understand about the test as a whole.

Most students should write the test at least twice. If you can make an improvement then that shows perseverance, which is beneficial to your application. Most schools don't require you to submit all test attempts, which means you should maximize your chance of getting a great score. For the few schools that do require you to submit all test scores, your score is considered to be your best score, not your worst. Some people are fearful of writing the test more than once. There is certainly an argument for not writing the test seven times – you should know that your ACT score is not the most important feature of your application. No school will admit you solely because you have a great test score! Writing the test three times is a good balance to even out statistical variation and ensure you maximize your score. In my experience, students do not improve much after their third test attempt, assuming they studied properly for the first three.

What is superscoring?

Superscoring is a process that some schools use to look at your ACT score if you have written it more than once. Let's say you wrote the ACT three times, and you got the following scores:

English	Math	Reading	Scientific Reasoning	Composite
28	24	29	25	27
29	27	26	30	28
28	28	28	29	28

Now, there's not much difference between those tests in terms of composite score, but for a school that superscores, they will take the highest score of each section. So that means 29 for English, 28 for Math, 29 for Reading and 30 for Scientific Reasoning. They would calculate your score as a 29. This doesn't give you any kind of advantage, because that particular school will do that for every applicant. However, it does mean that it is in your best interests to write the ACT more than once if you want to go to a school that superscores. It also means that when you are looking at that school's admissions profile to see if you are a good match, you should take a superscored version of your ACT score to compare with the admissions profile. Look up "does [school name] superscore the ACT" to find out.

What are subject tests, and should I take them?

Subject tests are administered by the College Board – the SAT organization. They are also known as SAT subject tests, or SAT IIs. They are tests of knowledge, not skill. This makes them different from the ACT or SAT. You'll find them like multiple-choice versions of what you have studied in school. They aren't required by many schools, but sometimes they can be an asset to your application if you're applying to competitive schools. Check the admissions pages of schools you're applying to, to see if they're required. If it says they're recommended, you should take them. You do these as well as the ACT or SAT, not instead of.

Index to Question Types

In this section, I've classified each of the questions in the five ACT online practice papers by type. This might help you if you feel that you are struggling with a particular type of question. The types I have classified these questions under are the same eight types we saw on page 30. Some questions fall into more than one category, so some numbers appear twice in the table. Go back through the tests you've done and write down the code (e.g. 67C - you can find these on the bottom left of each page) for each paper, and the question numbers that you got wrong. Look at the list below and see whether your errors fall more into one category than others. If this is true, and you do indeed struggle with a certain type of question, here's what you should do: use the answer explanations to make sure you fully understand each individual question, and then make sure that you are especially careful with this type in future.

Question type	59F	61C
Read a single piece of data	1, 2, 8, 21, 25, 36	10, 14, 29, 32, 35
Read or link two or more pieces of data	13, 15, 22, 37	2, 11, 36, 39
Identify trends, extrapolate, interpolate	3, 19, 20, 24, 31, 32	8, 9, 12, 15, 20, 21, 22, 23, 25, 27, 28, 30, 37, 38
Give a reason, cause or interpretation	4, 5, 6, 7, 9, 10, 11, 12, 18, 23, 24, 26, 27, 28, 34, 35, 38, 39, 40	3, 4, 5, 6, 7, 13, 18, 19, 26, 28, 31, 34, 40
Identify the variables, discuss the experiment design	14, 16, 17, 29, 30, 33, 34,	16, 33
Visualize the experimental set-up	23	
Answer from your own knowledge	40	17
Calculate/identify the equation		1, 24, 29, 35

Question type	64E	67C
Read a single piece of data	1, 3, 6, 19, 22, 28, 35, 40	13, 18, 19, 24, 36
Read or link two or more pieces of data	4, 5, 7, 12, 13, 17, 23, 36	1, 7, 8, 21, 25, 38
Identify trends, extrapolate, interpolate	8, 9, 21, 24	11, 14, 16, 20, 31, 32, 33, 40

Give a reason, cause or inter-pretation	2, 10, 14, 15, 16, 21, 25, 27, 29, 30, 31, 33, 34, 37, 38, 39	2, 5, 6, 9, 10, 15, 17, 19, 23, 26, 29, 30, 32, 33, 34, 35, 37, 39[1]
Identify the variables, discuss the experiment design	11, 26	3, 4, 12, 22
Visualize the experimental set-up	32, 40	
Answer from your own knowl-edge	18, 20	24, 28, 34, 35
Calculate/identify the equa-tion		27

Question type	1572-CPRE
Read a single piece of data	10, 15, 18, 19, 23, 40
Read or link two or more piec-es of data	1, 8, 9, 13, 22
Identify trends, extrapolate, interpolate	4, 16, 25, 26, 31, 39
Give a reason, cause or inter-pretation	2, 5, 11, 12, 17, 20, 29, 32, 33, 34, 36, 38
Identify the variables, discuss the experiment design	3, 6, 7, 27, 28, 30, 35, 37
Visualize the experimental set-up	
Answer from your own knowl-edge	14, 21, 34
Calculate/identify the equa-tion	24

(Footnotes)

1   This is my least favorite question ever on the ACT Scientific Reasoning!! If you're confused about it, see the answer explanation.

33627952R00073

Made in the USA
San Bernardino, CA
24 April 2019